FAITH UNDER PRESSURE

BY PAM GIBBS

LifeWay Press®
Nashville, Tennessee

ISBN: 9781415870037
Item Number: 005387851

Dewey Decimal Classification Number: 227.91
Subject Heading:
BIBLE. N.T. JAMES--STUDY \ CHRISTIAN LIFE \ FAITH

Printed in the United States of America

Student Ministry Publishing
LifeWay Church Resources
One LifeWay Plaza
Nashville, TN 37234-0174

We believe that the Bible has God for its author; salvation for its end; and truth, without any mixture
of error, for its matter and that all Scripture is totally true and trustworthy. The 2000 statement of *The
Baptist Faith and Message* is our doctrinal guideline.

✳ Contents

✳ About the author

Pam Gibbs technically serves as the Girls' Ministry Specialist at LifeWay Christian Resources, although her coworkers know she's *actually* the resident practical joker. She has worked at LifeWay since 1999, becoming the Girls' Ministry Specialist in 2008. She is also the author of several Bible studies, including *Girl Talk: The Power of Your Words* and *Esther: The Role of a Lifetime.*

Pam is a native Texan who became a Christian at youth camp when she was 13. She has a heart for students and began working in student ministry at age 19. She graduated from Wayland Baptist University (where she was a disc jockey and even took a class in roller skating) before getting her Masters of Divinity at Southwestern Baptist Theological Seminary.

After moving to Nashville, she went on a blind date with a high school teacher and coach named Jim, whom she married in 2002. Jim and Pam adopted a baby girl, Kaitlyn, from Guatemala in 2006.

Pam loves to be on the go and enjoys traveling for work. She's not afraid to be adventurous—she has the scars from sports injuries and their resulting surgeries on her knees to prove it. Her dream is to scuba dive off the Great Barrier Reef in Australia before she dies, although she'll need to learn how to scuba dive first.

What's this study all about?

Imagine that you're looking online for a full-time summer job. You type in the city and state where you live, hit enter, and wait for a list of amazing opportunities that will not only give you great experience but will also pay very well. (Yeah, right, like THAT'S gonna happen.) Hoping against hope, you begin to scroll down the page. You read ad after ad for every fast food restaurant imaginable.

But at the bottom of the page, something strange catches your eye. It reads:

> Learner wanted. Must be willing to endure ridicule from friends and painful hardship. Proper speech, discipline, humility, and patience also required. Mistreatment by others likely. Character will be severely tested. Success in program dependent upon relationship with the teacher. Apply only if you are willing to give up your life.

Of course you'd never see that ad. Because it's crazy.

But it's also the life of a Christian. That job description—that's what we're called to as believers.

It's not easy to be a follower of Jesus. But thankfully, He hasn't left us without help or asked us to figure everything out all by ourselves. The Book of James is about faith under pressure. It's about not giving in when you face trials and temptations. It's about being authentic and not just doing all the outward stuff that makes you look like a so-called "good Christian."

Over the next eight weeks, you will learn a lot about the practical stuff of being a follower of Jesus—like allowing your faith to lead to action, being at peace with God and others, taming your tongue, drawing near to God, and resisting the Devil. Your faith will be stretched. It's supposed to be stretched. That's the point. A faith that doesn't change and grow is dead.

You'll also discover some hard truths. Someone once said reading the Book of James is like being hit over the head with a 2-by-4 piece of wood. It hurts! But be encouraged, the same God who helped the first readers of this Letter will be right by your side, too, encouraging you and enabling you to put into practice the truths He reveals.

In the end, you'll discover that it's not easy being a follower of Jesus, but there's no better full-time job to take!

HOW TO USE THIS STUDY

Trials. Temptation. Favoritism. Peace. Authenticity.

Your faith collides with everyday life and you often wonder how to remain a faithful follower of Jesus in the midst of all that pressure. This eight-week study will help you learn that you can survive—and even thrive—when faith meets life.

This Bible study is a deeper type of study that focuses on the Book of James, a no-holds-barred, tell-it-like-it-is kind of book. James is all about the nuts and bolts of truly living out your faith in the real world, when it's easy and when you're facing pressures from every side. The Book of James helps us to understand that although living the life of faith will be tough at times—sometimes incredibly tough—true faith will endure—and even flourish.

Each week you will study a section of the Book of James or delve into James' life so that you will have context for the book. You will begin each week with a short introduction or overview of the week's theme, then dive into the first day of study. Each week will include five days of in-depth Bible study. Each day will end with a page called "Training Manual." Each week you will read through one chapter of James. On Day 1 of each week, you'll read James 1; on Day 2, you'll read James 2, and so on. The "Training Manual" pages will help you to process and evaluate what you're reading, while encouraging you to read it in light of the themes and topics you've studied that week. It will also challenge you to apply the Truths you find to your daily life.

In addition to reading a chapter of James each day, this study will also help you to develop the daily discipline of spending time in God's Word. The work is not difficult or time-consuming; it should only take 10-15 minutes to complete each day's work. Yes, I know you're busy, but really, what's 10-15 minutes? Give up a few minutes of TV-watching, texting, or mindless surfing on the Internet and invest in reading God's Word. I know you won't be sorry!

In addition to your personal study, you will also meet with a small group of girls and a leader (or leaders) each week for a more in-depth discussion of what God is teaching you. At each meeting, you'll discuss what God is teaching you and participate in deep discussions with your small group about the weeks' topics, themes, and what it all means for your daily life. You'll end each session with a time of prayer with the girls in your group.

The small group component of this study is important. You are going to be faced with difficult questions during these eight weeks and come face-to-face with hard truths in Scripture that will challenge you, convict you, and, I pray, change you. During this Bible study, you will examine your relationship with Christ to see if you really have one or if you're a Christian in name only. You will deal with tough topics, like temptation, suffering, prayer, and wisdom. And the girls in your small group are going through all of that right beside you. Be honest with them. Share your struggles and your victories and ask them to hold you accountable to what God calls you to do through your study of His Word. Be a trustworthy member of the group, remembering that what is shared in small group needs to stay there. Pray for the members of your small group and your leader, asking God to soften everyone's heart to what He has to say to each one of you. Participate in the group and get to know the girls who are walking through the Book of James with you. You have a unique opportunity to see the body of Christ working as it should in this small group—so don't miss out!

Finally, take James' words in James 1:22: "But be doers of the word and not hearers only, deceiving yourselves." Don't walk away from this study having gained a lot of knowledge, but never encountering Christ. Seek Him. Pray for the Holy Spirit's guidance. Grow deeper in love with Him and His Word through this study. Refuse to walk away unchanged.

The life of faith isn't easy, but it is absolutely worth it!

Faith Under Pressure: Possible

Knowing a little bit about an author can make a difference in how you understand what she writes. For instance, most everyone has heard of the Harry Potter series written by a woman named J.K. Rowling. You might even know that she was a single mother living on welfare when she wrote the first novel in the series.

What you probably don't know is this: J.K.'s mom passed away when she was only 25 years old, and her grief was great. This event affected her life so much that the theme of family and loss runs throughout all of her books. Everything just makes more sense now that you know the whole story, right?

The same applies to books in the Bible. Knowing that David, the singer, wrote many of the psalms, enriches your appreciation and understanding of his songs in the Book of Psalms. Or knowing that Luke was a physician might make you look at the healings he discusses in his Gospel a little differently.

That's why it's important that you know the whole story when it comes to the book we'll be studying for the next eight weeks: the Book of James. It was written by a real person with a real family. It is set in a real historical context with its own culture. Knowing this background can make a real difference in how you understand the book. That's why you'll be spending your first week of this study discovering everything you can about who James was and the world in which he lived, rather than diving right into the first chapter of the book that bears his name.

Context matters.

If you walked up to a group of friends and they all started laughing hysterically, your first thought would probably be, "Why are they laughing at me?"

But if you'd known the context of the situation—that someone had told a great joke right before you walked up—you would have been spared a lot of grief.

Or say you walk into the locker room and you start blabbing about your boyfriend's most annoying habit when your best friend suddenly bursts into tears. Would you have talked about your boyfriend if you had known your best friend had just seen her ex-boyfriend, whom she'd just broken up with a few days ago, hugging some other girl in the hall?

Context is important. It helps us to better understand situations, comments, and why people react to certain things the way they do. And context is also important when you're studying Scripture. That's why the first part of this Bible study is about context—the author, whom he was writing to, where they were living, what those people were facing, and what the world was like around them. Setting the Book of James in context will deepen your understanding and hopefully make this journey together a little bit richer.

So, who was James, this famous guy who wrote a book of the Bible?

Circle the answer you think is correct.

a) James the Younger (Mark 15:40)

b) James the son of Alphaeus, one of the 12 disciples (Matt. 10:3)

c) James, the father of one of the 12 disciples (Luke 6:16)

d) James, the brother of Jesus (Mark 6:3)

e) James, the brother of John and one of the 12 disciples (Matt. 10:2)

Theologians don't all agree on this (partially because it was such a common name), but most would say that the writer of this letter-turned-book-in-the-New Testament was James, the brother of Jesus. (Technically, though, James and Jesus were half-brothers since Jesus' mother was Mary, but His father was God.)

✱ WHO ARE YOU?

What do we know about this James?

Read John 7:2-5 to find out more, then consider the following questions.

✳ What did Jesus' brothers say to Him?

✳ Why do you think they gave Him such advice?

9

* What important thing do you learn about the brothers in verse 5?

If James didn't believe in Jesus initially, what changed in his heart? We get a glimpse in 1 Corinthians 15:1-8. Pay close attention to verse 7.

Read it and jot down a summary of what happened.

I have older siblings. We fought all the time growing up. We taunted each other, annoyed each other, and drove each other crazy, especially on long road trips to our grandmother's house (before the days of SUVs, portable DVD players, and iPods). Stuck in the back seat, the three of us tortured each other. We saw each other at our best—and at our absolute worst.
Jesus grew up with His brothers, learned His earthly father's trade alongside His brothers, ate with His brothers, and went to the synagogue with His brothers. They saw His actions—all the time. And yet, when Jesus began His public ministry, they didn't believe in Him. I wonder why?

James' heart may have been changed because Jesus appeared to him after the resurrection. I can't imagine what that encounter might have been like. James was probably doing the same things he had been doing before the crucifixion—working as a carpenter, taking care of his family, following the law as a good Jewish man would. But then—in an unlikely, unbelievable, unforgettable moment—His brother and yet somehow much more than just a brother—stood before Him in God's glory. Jesus had died. Everyone saw it. He'd been buried. And now He was standing in front of James very much alive. Wow. No wonder James became a believer.

* Do you have any thoughts about why Jesus' brothers didn't believe in Him at first? Write them below:

* What about you? What made you want to become a believer? What convinced you that the claims of Jesus were real and that you needed Him as Savior?

✱ NOW WHAT?

James' biography doesn't stop with him believing in Jesus. We learn a little about his life afterward.

Read Acts 12:6-17.

✳ What do you learn about James in these verses?

To understand James' life and place in history, you have to put yourself in first-century Jerusalem. For centuries, people had been following the Jewish law, waiting for the coming of a Messiah who would overthrow Rome and set up a kingdom on earth. That's what the Jews wanted. But that's not what they got. So there were many people who simply didn't believe in Jesus as the Messiah, their Savior.

But a few did believe. Then Jesus, the One they claimed was the Messiah, was crucified and buried. (I cannot imagine what that must have been like for them. It must have seemed like their worst nightmare had become reality.) And then, three days later, after seeing Jesus die, He appeared to them. Alive. In the flesh. Bearing the marks of the crucifixion, but very much living and breathing.

But He didn't stay with them for long.

Read Acts 1:4-14.

✳ What happened to Jesus in these few verses?

✳ What did He tell the people? Why is that important?

✳ Why would reporting the story to him be important?

✳ According to verses 12-14, who were among the believers gathered in Jerusalem soon after Jesus' resurrection?

✳ Scripture records that these early believers were "continually united in prayer." Why do you think they did this?

A small, unorganized, still-questioning, wondering, confused-yet-believing group of followers went back to Jerusalem, back to what they knew and understood, where they had lived and worked and prayed. But one thing was different. They followed a Messiah who wasn't exactly like the one they had been expecting for centuries. Instead of an earthly king who overthrew the Roman government, the Messiah had been killed on a cross, then rose from the dead (which would totally freak me out to begin with), and had just ascended into heaven right before their eyes.

And in middle of all that confusion and joy and hope and messiness, the Christian church was born. What we understand as a church—a group of believers who come together weekly in a building to listen to a preacher and pray and talk and sing praise choruses and hear from God— was not what those believers first experienced. Growing the church took a lot of time. And prayer. And work. And mistakes. And disagreements.

And as history records it, James, the brother of Jesus, became a major figure who was in the middle of it all, one of the leaders among the Christians of his day. That's why it was so important for the people to report the news to him. He was one of their leaders.

✱ ADD IT ALL UP

Based on all the information you've gathered in this short time, what can you recall about the person called James, the brother of Jesus? **Write down everything you can remember.**

Tomorrow, we'll learn more about James' character. But for now, meditate on this thought: *Even though James didn't even believe in Jesus until after His death and resurrection, God still used James to help form and establish the early church.* **What does that tell you about God and His character? Why should that matter to you?**

TRAINING MANUAL

Today, you'll read James 1. Use the following outline to guide your interaction with Scripture as the Holy Spirit speaks to you.

* Pray.

* Read the entire chapter.

* Paraphrase the major points of the chapter:

* What is God telling you about Himself through these verses?

* What is God telling you about yourself and/or others?

* How does God want you to respond to what He has said to you?

James, the slave

If you were to describe your relationship with God, what words would you use? Friend? Follower? Skeptic? Curious seeker?

List all the words, phrases, or adjectives you would use to describe your relationship with God.

I can be fairly certain that the word *slave* didn't make your list. Why, you ask? Because no one likes that word. The connotations are just too negative.

When you hear the word "slave," what pictures come to mind?

✳ JAMES, THE SLAVE

Imagine being held against your will, forced to work without pay, treated like an animal, being beaten, and living in poverty. Slavery is not a pretty picture, whether you're talking about slavery in America's history or slavery as it occurs today (yes, it is still a reality in many parts of the world). Yet, James used that very word to describe himself.

Find James 1:1 in your Bible and rewrite it in the space below. Then underline the word "slave" and circle to whom or what James claimed he was a slave.

Why would James use that term?

The term *slave* is totally foreign to us living in the United States today. No one would voluntarily write in an email or text message, "*I am a slave of . . .* " It just wouldn't happen! Our culture is opposed to any idea of enslavement. No one controls us, right?

The term is even more foreign to you as a teen. At this time in your life, you probably crave independence, to make your own decisions, to be on your own. You don't want anyone telling you what to do.

So what makes James so different from us? Why would James be willing to call himself a slave? Why didn't he care about his own freedom?

To answer those questions, read John 8:30-36.

✳ According to Jesus, how does a person become a slave?

* According to these verses, how does a person find true freedom?

* How do you think the Jewish people felt when Jesus informed them that they were slaves?

I would imagine that Jesus telling the Jewish people that they were slaves didn't do much for His popularity. Remember, their ancestors had spent their lives in slavery to Pharaoh until God delivered them. And the Jewish people took great pride in their so-called freedom and along comes this young, traveling teacher who tells them that they're really slaves to sin.

I don't know if James was in the crowd that day when Jesus talked about freedom and slavery. Perhaps Mary asked James to check on her firstborn Son. Maybe James was curious about whether people loved or hated his Brother. Or maybe he wasn't there at all. Either way, James became aware of one central, certain truth: **If your life is given to anything but Jesus, it's really not freedom at all. Sin takes us captive, and the only thing that can set us free is Jesus.**

✳ YOU, A SLAVE?

Stop for a minute and think about your own life and the things that captivate you. Anything that drives your actions, anything that you can't live without or that dominates your thoughts and feelings—those are the things to which you are a slave.

Look at the list below. Underline those things that hold you captive now. Circle those things that have enslaved you in the past. Remember—anything that dominates your life is your master, and you are its slave.

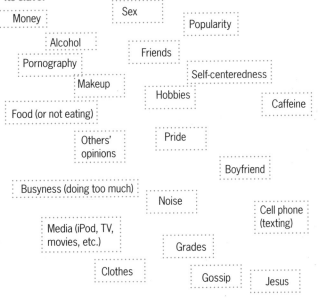

Money   Sex   Popularity
Alcohol   Friends
Pornography   Self-centeredness
Makeup   Hobbies   Caffeine
Food (or not eating)
Others' opinions   Pride   Boyfriend
Busyness (doing too much)   Noise   Cell phone (texting)
Media (iPod, TV, movies, etc.)   Grades
Clothes   Gossip   Jesus

Which master enslaves you the most? How do you know?

Why did James call himself a slave? Because giving yourself over to God is better than any life of so-called "freedom" you could have apart from Him. *(Hint: If you're apart from God, you don't really have freedom.)* Nothing else satisfies. Nothing else completes. Nothing else can set you free to become the person God designed you to be when He created you.

✱ DYING TO LIVE

So, what happened to James? Truthfully, nobody knows for sure how he died. Some historians think he was stoned to death for political reasons.

Another story goes like this: The Jewish leaders were afraid that the people would continue to follow Jesus as the Messiah and would be led astray. They recognized James as a leader among the people, and so during the Passover time in Jerusalem, they asked him to tell the people to pack up, go home, get on with their lives, and not get crazy over the guy named Jesus (that's a modern way to say it). Instead, when he was confronted in the temple, he stood up and said, "Why do you ask me concerning the Son of Man? He is now sitting in Heaven at the right hand of the Most High and will come on the clouds of Heaven."[1]

According to this story, when the Jewish leaders heard this, they went berserk and threw him down the steps of the temple, intending to kill him (some scholars think he was actually on the top of the temple at the time). When he didn't die in the fall, he was struck in the head and killed, probably around 62 A.D.

No one really knows exactly how he died. But there is one common thread that's apparent in all the stories about James' death: he died because of his connection to Jesus. James became one of the first Christian martyrs, that much is clear.

James' life took some dramatic turns—from thinking Jesus was out of His mind (Mark 3:21) to encountering Jesus after the resurrection, to becoming a leader in the early church, to calling himself Jesus' slave, to dying because of his radical, powerful, unshakable belief in Jesus.

And the great news for you and me is that the same God who transformed James' life can transform ours, too, wherever we are on the journey.

Sources:
1. John Foxe, *Foxe's Book of Martyrs* (New Kensington, Penn.: Whitaker House, 1981), 11.

TRAINING MANUAL

Today, you'll read James 2. Use the following outline to help guide your interaction with Scripture as the Holy Spirit speaks to you.

* Pray.

* Read the entire chapter.

* Paraphrase the major points of this chapter:

* What is God telling you about Himself through these verses?

* What is God telling you about yourself and/or others?

* How does God want you to respond to what He has said to you?

✳ A letter to the people, part 1

If you send a text message to your friends, the way it sounds will be dramatically different than an essay you write for college entrance exams. LOL and CUL8R work when you are saying good night to your crush. It's not OK to put in an English paper. The recipient of your communication will dictate what you write and how you write it.

The same truth applies to the Book of James. Many of the books in the New Testament are actually letters written from church leaders (like Paul or John) with specific people in specific circumstances. James had a specific audience in mind when he wrote his letter.

Read James 1:1. To whom was James writing? Copy your answer from the Scripture.

You should have written something like, *the twelve tribes scattered among the nations (NIV)* or *to the 12 tribes in the Dispersion* (HCSB). Both of those answers are correct, but they don't really help much, do they? Just who were the Jewish Christians scattered across the nations? Why would James use the phrase "twelve tribes" to describe them? Why were they scattered across the nations? And, most of all, why does any of that matter to you, living in the 21st century?

✱ A LITTLE HISTORY LESSON

You might know more than you think you do. Think about all that you have learned during your time in Sunday School.

Where does this reference to 12 tribes come from? Can you think back? Jot down any information you can recall:

Let's look in Scripture to jog your memory and see if you can remember some more.

Read Exodus 1:1-5.

✳ List all of the family members who went to Egypt with their father, Jacob:

Did you get 12 sons? Reuben, Simeon, Levi, Judah, Issachar, Zebulun, Benjamin, Dan, Naphtali, Gad, Asher, and of course, Joseph. These are the 12 sons of Jacob. Why is that important? You need to go back a little further in Scripture to discover that answer.

Read Genesis 25:21-26. List the principal characters in this story:

Father:

Mother:

Firstborn son:

Second son:

Put them into the order, oldest to youngest.

Oldest:

Youngest:

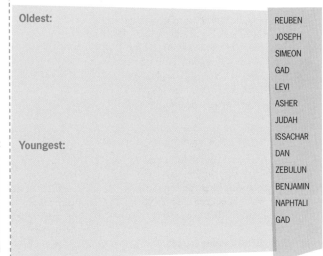

REUBEN
JOSEPH
SIMEON
GAD
LEVI
ASHER
JUDAH
ISSACHAR
DAN
ZEBULUN
BENJAMIN
NAPHTALI
GAD

This is the story of the birth of Esau and Jacob. (Remember Jacob? He was the one with 12 sons.) So Jacob's father is Isaac. Who was Isaac's father? And why does this matter to you? Why are you doing ancient history when you could be playing Wii? Hang on a little longer and you'll see why it matters.

Read Genesis 21:1-6. List the principle characters in this story:

Father:

Mother:

Son:

Like puzzle pieces that fit together to create a picture, this story completes the history. Put them all into place. Below are the names of the important people (for our purposes) from the passages of Scripture you just looked up.

So here's how the family history plays out. Abraham was the eldest, followed by Isaac who had two sons—Esau and Jacob. Jacob and his wives ended up with 12 sons. Yes, 12 boys. Can you imagine the stinky boy funk in that household—in a culture without body wash and deodorant?

✴ A PROMISE FULFILLED

Long before those 12 boys were born, God made a promise to their great-grandfather, a promise that they would not forget—nor would their children or grandchildren.

Read Genesis 12:1-7.

✴ What was that promise?

God told Abram (later Abraham) to leave his home country and to go to a place he'd never been before. Being obedient, he took his wife (Sarai/Sarah) and his nephew Lot and set out for the land of Canaan. (Check in the back of your Bible to see if you have a map of that journey. Mine does, and it shows me how long this journey was!) And when they arrived, God promised to give that land to his offspring, or his future family—his children, grandchildren, and so forth. So what happened? For a while, nothing. But later on . . .

Read Exodus 1:1-14.

* Where were Jacob and his 12 sons (well, 11—Joseph was already there) headed?

* What happened once they arrived?

* Who took note of this increasingly growing family?

* Why was he worried?

* What did he do about it?

Yep. This is where the family and lineage of Jacob (thousands upon thousands by now) became enslaved in Egypt. The sons of Abraham had been promised a vast land, the land of Canaan. And here they were, living under the harsh, cruel, unbearable conditions of slavery in Egypt. So God sent a deliverer—Moses. And you probably know the rest of the story.

This million-man (and women and children) march around Egypt for 40 years finally ended with the death of Moses and the appointment of Joshua as the man who would lead them back, hundreds of years later, to the land God had promised to them. The land of Canaan, the land "flowing with milk and honey" (Ex. 3:8), a land also called Israel or Palestine.

The promised land wasn't huge. West of the Jordan River, it covered approximately 6,000 square miles. East of the Jordan, an area of about 4,000 square miles was included in the land of Israel. In all, this land was about the size of Massachusetts (which is 10,555 square miles) or Vermont (which is 9,615 square miles). To give you some perspective, Texas is 268,580 square miles.

When they finally got back to this relatively small tract of land, it took them several years to divide up the promised land and settle. (Check out Joshua 14–19 if you want the details of which family group got what part of Palestine.) So they were finally home. But not permanently.

Eventually, this promised land was split in two: the Northern Kingdom and the Southern Kingdom. And, the people from both parts of Israel had a great propensity to rebel against God and suffer the consequences—great consequences. Time after time, they fell prey to outside forces, like the Midianites, the Philistines, the Ammonites, and eventually the Babylonians.

Read 2 Kings 17:6-7.

✴ What happened in these verses? Write a short outline below.

That's the Northern Kingdom (10 tribes). And just for reference, that happened in about 722 B.C.

After reading what happened to the Jews in the north, you may be wondering how the Southern Kingdom was faring around the same time. To know more about that, you have to read a little more from 2 Kings.

Read what happened to Jerusalem (considered the most important city among the Jewish people) in 2 Kings 25:1-12.

✴ What happened to King Zedekiah? The temple? The city walls?

✴ What happened to the Jews who were living in the land at the time?

✴ What happened to most of the people? (See v. 11.)

✳ What happened to the city itself? Draw what you think that looked like.

That's right, the Jewish people were scattered away from their homeland, the land of Israel, also known as the promised land. This is what is called "The Diaspora" or "The Dispersion." This was a continual process, beginning around 722 B.C. for the people in the northern part of Israel (most of them were resettled in Assyria), and in 586 B.C., when the people of the Southern Kingdom experienced the same fate and were transported to Babylon. While some of these people later returned to Judah, many of them remained permanently in Babylon. Later, other wars fought by the Greeks and Romans helped scatter more of the Jewish people. No longer were the children of God living in one central location; they were scattered abroad.

Tomorrow, we'll tackle those questions lingering in the back your mind: *Why are we reviewing this history? What does this have to do with the Book of James? And how could this possibly connect with my life?*

But for now, ask yourself one question: **What would I have done if I had been taken away from home to live in a foreign country against my will?**

TRAINING MANUAL

Today, you'll read James 3. Use the following outline to help guide your interaction with Scripture as the Holy Spirit speaks to you.

* Pray.

* Read the entire chapter.

* What is God telling you about Himself through these verses?

* Paraphrase the major points of this chapter:

* What is God telling you about yourself and/or others?

* How does God want you to respond to what He has said to you?

A letter to the people, part 2

Yesterday, we ended with a tough question: What would you have done if you'd been forced to leave your home and live in a foreign country? Put yourself in that person's sandals for a minute.

You're a 5th-century-B.C. Jew. It's bedtime. You've blown out the flame from the last lamp for the night. You lie in the dark next to your spouse. Then you hear it. A scream. Then another. Suddenly, chaos erupts outside your window. You hear the shuffle of feet. The thump of fists slamming into flesh. You and your husband fly out of bed and spring to the door. You open it, and standing before you is a soldier, sword drawn and ready to strike. He grabs you by the hair and your husband by his neck. Your husband is slammed onto a cart stuffed full of men his age—some bleeding, some unconscious, some numb with shock. You are shoved into another group of young women, then forced into another cart and carried away in the night, under the cover of darkness and fear. After a very long journey with little water and even less food, you begin to see the outcroppings of buildings in shapes unfamiliar to you. You begin to see people, but even they look different. They speak a different language. You are forced out of the cart, into a stall like a pig, and held captive until you are again shuffled into another group of young women, awaiting an unknown fate.

In that moment, what are you feeling? What are you thinking? What options do you have? How would you describe your feelings toward God during that experience? Write about them below.

Anger. Fear. Confusion. Uncertainty. Anguish. Grief. And yet, in the midst of all of that, the Jewish people who had been taken away from their homeland had a few choices. They could continue to rely on their faith in Yahweh, the God of their fathers and forefathers and other ancestors. They could keep hope alive and believe that one day, God would bring them back to their homes, back to the center of their family and faith and all things familiar, back to the land God had promised them. They could choose to rebel against their captors and find themselves killed. Or, they could just blend in.

Believe it or not, this isn't the first time someone in the Old Testament faced a decision like this. Scripture tells us that a teenager named Daniel was faced with a very similar choice.

Read Daniel 1:1-8 to find out his story.

✳ What was to happen to the Jews from the royal family and nobility?

* What were they to learn?

* What was to happen after three years?

* What did Daniel decide to do, according to verse 8?

That famous story of Daniel choosing not to eat the meat is an example of someone who chose not to fit in with the foreign culture, including their gods and their religion. But what does this history lesson mean for you? That's the real question, isn't it? You're not a Jew living in Babylon (modern-day Iraq), so what's the point?

Here's the answer: You are them. You are just like the Jewish people scattered across the globe.

The dispersed Jews lived in a culture that didn't follow the God of Scripture. So do you. In fact, the surrounding culture was full of false gods. So is yours. The Jews in the centuries before Christ's birth had to choose between their faith and their comfort. So do you. They struggled to keep their identity as a nation, as God's own people. So do you—as a follower of Jesus.

By the time Jesus died and rose again, as many Jews lived outside of Palestine as lived inside the land. In almost every city Paul visited on his missionary journeys, he found a Jewish synagogue (Acts 14:1; 17:1,10; 18:4). Why does that matter? Because even though such a displacement must have been painful for the families affected, God worked things together for His good (Rom. 8:28). This transport of Jewish people from their home to other countries helped pave the way for the spread of the gospel.

And just as God used the dispersion of His people to foreign cultures, God wants to use you to be a light in a dark world as you are faithful to Him, too. You will be a beacon in a very dark place when you don't accept the gods of your culture, such as money, popularity, beauty, self-satisfaction, instant gratification, and sex.

You can choose to blend in, adopt the customs of this culture, and give your life over to things that this society has to offer. But if you make that choice, you'll become less than what God designed you to be. God has a plan and a purpose for you that far exceeds anything that this world can offer you. A life with God is better than anything you could find outside of Him.

✳ WHY THE TWELVE TRIBES?

We're still left with the question: Why in the world would James call these Jewish Christians "the twelve tribes"? And how do we know James was even writing to Christians?

Let's answer the last question first. To do that, we'll read one simple verse:

Read James 2:1.

✳ What did James call the people to who he was writing? Write it below.

He calls them brothers and believers in Jesus. That settles one of our questions.

So what about the 12 tribes? Seems kind of an odd, obscure reference for new Jews who believed in Jesus. Why not call them saints or beloved or new creations or any of the other dozens of terms that the New Testament uses to refer to Christians?

There is no ironclad explanation. There's no YouTube interview with James that tells us the answer, no search engine on the Internet to look up the answer. So this is just a suggestion, just an idea formed in my brain as I'm sitting in my office thinking about what it would be like to be a first-century Jewish Christian.

I think it would be lonely.

Remember, the church as we know it today with a youth ministry, a choir, a pastor, and a building didn't exist. Not yet, anyway. These first-century Christians didn't just pass the plate, build a sanctuary, and start outreach programs. These were people who had been a part of a centuries-old religion, a piece of a legacy that had been communicated to them from their parents and their parents' parents and their parents . . . you get the picture. Being a Jew brought a sense of identity and shared community, vision, and purpose.

But if you were a Jew who chose to believe in Jesus as the Messiah, where did that leave you? Were you still a part of a community of faith? Did you have an identity? A vision? A purpose? The short answer is yes.

I think James brought up the 12 tribes as a way to remind the people that they still had a history. They shared a common story, a story of faith that began in Abraham but found its ultimate fulfillment in Jesus Christ. They needed to be reminded that they were still family—a bit different than what they had been taught about as children, but still a family.

Why do I think they needed reminding? Because I hear it again in James 2:1. What does he call the people? Brothers (he also calls them "brothers" in 2:5 and 2:14). Family. And when you're a small family (like Jewish Christians living across the world), every member matters. They had been transferred from one family (Jewish culture, tradition, and religion of their history) to another—the family of faith.

And like every family, the first-century Jewish Christians struggled. They disagreed with each other. They showed favoritism. They argued. They let their speech go in the wrong direction. They were tempted by the Devil.

How do I know? Because all of those subjects (and more) are part of the Book of James.

✱ WHAT ABOUT YOU?

You are just like those early Christians. No, you probably don't come from a Jewish background. But you still share some common ground.

Look back at the last two paragraphs on page 26. Circle the things the early believers struggled with. Then, list in the space below (or draw or whatever) the things that you struggle with now.

For now, end this day thinking about what you've learned the last two days. Reflect on how much you are like the Jewish Christians to whom James wrote. Then, journal your thoughts and feelings in the space provided below.

See? You have a lot more in common with people in the first century than you thought. And tomorrow, you'll discover that the religious climate of their day was a lot like what you face every time you walk down the halls of your school or turn on your TV.

Here's the really cool thing: Just as the Jewish people shared a common heritage—a shared story that could be told across centuries—you have a shared history, too. As a believer, there are millions of faithful followers who have walked this journey of faith throughout history (Heb. 12:1). And there are millions who follow today. You may feel alone—much like those early Christians felt—but you are not. You are a part of an unbreakable chain, an eternal family. And you are not alone.

Welcome home.

TRAINING MANUAL

WEEK
1

Today, you'll read James 4. Use the following outline to help guide your interaction with Scripture as the Holy Spirit speaks to you.

✳ Pray.

✳ Read the entire chapter.

✳ What is God telling you about Himself in this chapter of James?

✳ Paraphrase the major points of this chapter:

✳ What is God telling you about yourself and/or others in these verses?

✳ What steps will you take this week to respond to what He has said to you through this passage of Scripture?

Life in the first century

Just for fun, spend a few minutes trying to identify what was popular in particular time in history. Match the "in" thing with the correct time frame.

1. The Betty Boop cartoon   A. 1920s

2. Disco music   B. 1930s

3. Poodle skirts   C. 1970s

4. Marbles   D. 1950s

5. Camera phone   E. 1960s

6. Beanie Babies   F. 1970s

7. Lava lamps   G. 1980s

8. The Charleston dance   H. 1990s

9. The Bee Gees   I. 1940s

10. Pop Rocks® (candy)   J. 2000s

(Check the leader's helps in the back for the answers if you need them. But no peeking before you at least try to match them up!)

Was that little game hard for you? Did you struggle? I bet you did, probably more so the further back in time you had to go. And that's just in the last hundred years or so! Can you imagine trying to identify what was popular in first-century Jerusalem, where James probably lived at the time the letter we're studying was written? Of course not! It's not tucked away in your brain behind the latest "American Idol" winner or the names of the Twilight characters. But understanding what the culture was like back in James' day is critical for us to understand his letter. If we don't have the background (the context, remember?), we'll miss out on the richer meaning and significance that it can bring to our lives.

✱ WHAT DO YOU PICTURE?

When you think about what life was like in the first-century Palestine (or Israel), what comes to mind?

Draw or write down everything you think of, using the following categories to guide your brainstorming.

Religion   Economy

Family

Transportation

Language

Sports/ Entertainment   Education   Food

Just so you'll have a little background, here's a little information about what life was like in the first century.

As you're reading through the list, circle the things that the world of first-century Israel shares with the culture of today.

WEEK
1

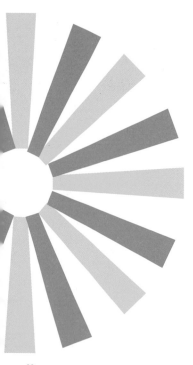

FAMILY
The family was the center of the social structure with the husband as the spiritual and legal representative; multiple generations of family and extended family lived together in one house (or in additions to an original house)

FOOD
Staple food consisted of bread, cheese, fruits, nuts, and mostly fish or chicken. Pork was considered unclean (and off-limits) for Jews.

LANGUAGE
The common language in the Roman Empire was Greek. However, at the time it was common for Jews to also use Hebrew, Aramaic, and Latin. Jesus' everyday language was Aramaic.

GOVERNMENT
The Roman Empire controlled most of the known world. Many local governing entities were allowed relative freedom, but always under the eye of the larger empire. Jews resisted Roman rule and longed for a Messiah who would overthrow the government and set up a kingdom on earth.

ECONOMY
The economy was supported by three major elements: agriculture (olives, dates, vineyards, grains, and so forth), trade spurred by the close proximity to the Mediterranean Sea, and large building projects. There was a large disparity between the rich and the poor.

EDUCATION
For a Jew, religion, law, ethics, and education went hand-in-hand. There was no separation of any element. Each informed and affected the other. Greeks focused on science, arts, language, and physical training.

SPORTS/ENTERTAINMENT
In Rome, track and field became popular, as did wrestling and boxing. Early board games included early versions of chess, checkers, and backgammon.

Did you notice one category is missing? That's because we'll be looking a little more closely at the religions of the first century. That's the part of this story that carries the most significance for you and me.

Scripture Reference	Greek God	Roman God	Function
Acts 14:8-13			
Acts 19:23-28			
Acts 28:11			

Castor & Pollux (Gemini)
Zeus
goddess of the hunt, wild animals, and the wilderness

Artemis
king of the gods, ruler of the sky and weather
Diana

Castor & Pollux (Dioskouroi)
patrons of sailors
Jupiter

✱ THE GODS THEY SERVED

If you've had to study mythology in school, you might have learned that the Greeks and Romans believed in the same gods, but they had different names. We know from Scripture that many people believed in these gods during early New Testament times.

Look at the chart and information above. Match the Scripture reference to the god referenced (you might need to use several translations to find all the names). Also, match both the Greek and Roman names for these gods, as well as the role or function they played.

You may need the help of your computer, iPad, or smart phone to complete the picture.

✱ ANCIENT GODS AND GODDESSES

In your literature or history class, you might have learned that Greek and Roman mythology said there were 12 main or major gods and goddesses that ruled the earth—the "Twelve Olympians." However, there were countless (literally) other gods who ruled over a family, a village or even a stream. Gods (with a little *g*) were everywhere, and each was to be honored, worshiped, and appeased. Making gods happy was a lifelong pursuit of the Roman and Greek people, and it was done by making sacrifices to the gods, holding festivals in a god's honor, establishing temples for worship, and other similar acts of tribute.

And if following all of those gods and their festivals and rites and temples wasn't confusing enough, a first-century man or woman could always add in the gods from other countries, like the goddess Isis from Egypt. Combined, this fragmented quagmire of rituals, superstitions, philosophy, and traditions left people in a state of confusion and dissatisfaction.

So how did these religious practices affect the Jewish people? And how did the larger Greek and Roman cultures relate to these people who were "little Christs," the new Christians who chose to follow one God instead of many? And just as importantly, why does this background on religions affect you as you study James?

That's a good question.

✱ US AND THEM

Confusion. Disillusionment. Polytheism (belief in many gods). A skewed worldview. Opposing lifestyles. A need for truth. Sounds a lot like the world of the first-century person, doesn't it?

But it also describes the people in your world right now—many of your friends, classmates, coworkers, and teammates. It may even describe you. While you are separated from that culture by about 2,000 years, you face problems that are remarkably similar to fellow Christians in the first century. They had to decide whether or not to participate in festivals to honor those hundreds of gods—festivals that took place every month. Not an issue for you, right? What if I reframed the situation like this: Have you ever struggled with whether or not to go to a party on a Friday night, wanting to fit in with your friends but not wanting be associated with the bad things at parties? You have more in common with early Christians than you thought.

The people James wrote to were often ridiculed for their faith in the one true God instead of participating in the cultural or state-mandated worship. Sound familiar? It should. While our country doesn't force you to bow down to a certain god, you still must choose whom or what you will follow, and drawing that line in the sand for Christ will draw criticism and even ridicule. In James' day there were so many gods, temples, superstitions and beliefs that the people were confused about what to believe. It's no different for you now. Without a strong relationship with Jesus, you could easily be confused by the philosophies, worldviews, and religions that permeate the hallways at your school, the music you listen to, and the movies you watch.

Not only will the Book of James challenge you, but it will also be your companion on your faith journey. Realizing that others have walked the same road you have will make the trip a little less scary and a lot less lonely.

And remember, you have your fellow believers and followers of the Truth to encourage and challenge you. Let's walk together on that journey through James—and through life.

TRAINING MANUAL

Today, you'll read James 5. Use the following outline to help guide your interaction with Scripture as the Holy Spirit speaks to you.

* Pray.

* Read the entire chapter.

* Paraphrase the major points of this chapter:

* What is God telling you about Himself in these verses?

* What is God telling you about yourself and/or others in this chapter of James?

* What specific steps will you take this week to respond to what has taught you through this passage of Scripture? List three steps below.

UNWAVERING

Faith Under Pressure: Unwavering

There's just something unique about visiting Magic Kingdom® at Walt Disney World®.

The minute you walk into the amusement park, it's like you've stepped into another world. A world full of princesses, castles, and music. Beasts and their beauties. A silly old bear and his Christopher Robin. In the Magic Kingdom, little girls become princesses, and little boys turn into pirates. It really does seem like the happiest place on earth—a place where there's no mounting deficit, no wars in the Middle East, and no political lobbyists peddling their brand of truth.

This year, I got to take my almost 6-year-old daughter to that magical place for the first time. She was enraptured. She got to meet characters from books, ride the teacups with her Grammy, and stay in a hotel with giraffes grazing outside her window. Nothing could have been better.

Until we came home.

We had to come back to real life—where friends say hurtful things, dogs run away, and mean people sometimes go to jail. No one can stay in Magic Kingdom forever.

This week, you'll discover that life is no trip to Magic Kingdom. Life isn't perfect; most of the time it's just hard. Tough stuff happens. People will hurt you. Your life will get turned upside down by situations you never expected.

But you'll also discover that while the kings in the fairy tales are just imaginary, the King who rules over the world is real, and He rules over every circumstance and trial you'll ever face.

Jesus meant it when He said He would be with you "always" (Matt. 28:20).

 Ready or not, here they come!

Some words just don't go together in the same sentence. For example, the phrase *chocolate-covered* should never be next to the word *ants*. It's just wrong. And so are these: *pretty ugly, seriously funny, old news, crash landing, hot chili,* and *jumbo shrimp*. And one that I will never get: *sweet tart.*

Today's Scripture passage contains words that just don't seem to go together, especially when you're going through a rough time. But God often does the unusual (like speaking through talking donkeys, having dry land under the Red Sea, and coming to earth as a Baby), so this passage sort of fits in with His character.

Read James 1:2-4.

✳ What are your initial thoughts about these verses? What sticks out to you?

✳ What strange combinations of words do you notice?

My Bible reads this way: "Consider it a great joy . . . whenever you experience various trials" (v. 2, HCSB).

Seriously? Has James lost his mind? When I'm going through a hard time, the last thought on my mind is, "Oh, I can consider this a great joy!" Most of the time, I'm busy trying to figure out what I did wrong to deserve such a hardship and how to get past it as quickly as possible. What in the world was James trying to tell us? A little digging may help answer that question.

✳ LOOKING FORWARD

First, you and I need to understand a little Greek. The word *joy* in James 1 doesn't literally mean *be joyful in the moment you are hurting*. James wasn't telling his readers to ignore or deny their difficult circumstances. Instead, the word *joy* as James uses it has the eternal end in mind. It means that you and I can find joy and hope in the end result of our present suffering. We know that there is a good end coming out of the trial, so we fix our focus and our joy on that, not on the immediate circumstances, as tough as they may be.

Read verses 3-4 again.

✳ According to these verses, what good can come out of trials?

✳ What is the ultimate result—the final end—of all of the trials we face?

Verse 3 tells us the outcome of our trials. We gain endurance. Think for a moment about the word *endurance*.

* What sorts of things would you need endurance to accomplish?

Maybe you listed some sort of athletic activity. If so, you're on the same track (no pun intended) as James was when he wrote these verses. Think of it like this: as a believer, you're like an athlete in training and each trial you go through builds your spiritual muscles, so to speak. Those trials produce commitment, consistency, and a faith that does not waver or give up. That faith is complete or mature. It's a faith in God that's fully grown and fully devoted. It's not going anywhere, no matter what happens. But the key to enduring life's most painful trials—and this is important to remember—is in looking forward to that end, not just focusing on the immediate pain. This kind of faith and endurance is a lifelong pursuit, not an instant transformation.

* REAL-LIFE EXAMPLE

When I moved to Nashville, my life began to fall into place like I'd always dreamed. I was blessed with a great job that played on my strengths. I found a church that I loved. And in a couple of years, I found him—the man I would spend the rest of my life with. We began to plan how we would spend this married life together. We planned our wedding and all its details.

Then everything started to fall apart. Two months (to the day, in fact) before we got married, my older sister died. And then, when we got off the plane from our honeymoon, we got into a car and went straight to the hospital, where my new father-in-law lay sick without a cause. We would later find out the name of that disease—cancer. He died two years after our marriage. In the middle of grieving his loss, my husband and I tried to have children but couldn't. So add that pain on top of the others. We pursued adoption, but had to endure a "failed match" (we were matched with a child, but later could not adopt her). A few months later, we found out that our (future) daughter was born. Six days later, my mother died.

That summarizes the first five years of my married life. Three deaths of close family members, infertility, and a failed adoption. And I will fully admit that in the midst of that pain—and grief, confusion, anger, desperation, and absolute desolation—the very last thing on my mind was joy in the moment.

My only goal was survival.

* LOOKING TO SCRIPTURE

What kept me going during those painful trials was choosing not to focus on the immediate circumstances. I won't say that was easy, because it wasn't. Those years were hard and painful, full of struggles and doubts. I had to go back to Scripture many times and look for the promises of God in the middle of my struggles, to be reminded of who He was and what He could do. One of my favorite passages of Scripture during that time was 2 Corinthians 4:16-18. Read it below. Underline all of the promises you find in these verses.

"So we're not giving up. How could we! Even though on the outside it often looks like things are falling apart on us, on the inside, where God is making new life, not a day goes by without his unfolding grace. These hard times are small potatoes compared to the coming good times, the lavish celebration prepared for us. There's far more here than meets the eye. The things we see now are here today, gone tomorrow. But the things we can't see now will last forever."
—2 Corinthians 4:16-18, *The Message*

✳ What promises did you discover in those verses? List them in your own words below:

✳

✳

✳

✳

✳

✳

✳

This passage is only one example of dozens of promises God makes to us. Read the following Scriptures and list the promise or promises in each.

✳ John 16:20-22

✳ 1 Corinthians 15:58

✳ Philippians 3:8-9

✳ Philippians 4:19

✳ James 1:12

✱ YOUR OWN STORY

You **will** face hard times. Scripture says "whenever" you face trials, not "if" you face them (v. 2). In fact, chances are, you've already had your fair share (or an unfair share) of difficult circumstances in your life. By remembering those times—especially how God used them for your growth and maturity—will help you when you face a new trial.

In the space provided, journal about a time you faced a trial or testing of sorts. The situation doesn't have to be huge; a fight with your best friend can be the laboratory for your growth. Or you may have faced trials that most of us have never had to endure. Whatever comes to mind, write it down in the space provided. **Also write down any promises you clung to in the midst of your trial.**

✱ TWO LAST WORDS

One last word of encouragement today: You may be in the middle of a fierce storm as you read this. And in that storm of life, it's pretty hard to think clearly. Everything is upside down. You feel like this hard time is never going to get any better. You may be on the verge of giving up. You may even feel abandoned by God. That's OK. What you feel is real, but it may not be reality. Your circumstances won't tell you what's true about God. Your feelings aren't necessarily the truth.

Take heart! This storm will not last forever. You will see the sun again. And when you do, you'll see that the Father was as close as your next breath. Joy will come—maybe not as quickly or as easily as you hope—but joy will come (Ps. 30:5).

TRAINING MANUAL

WEEK
2

Today, you'll read through James 1 again. Use the following outline to help guide your interaction with Scripture as the Holy Spirit speaks to you.

* Pray.

* Read the entire chapter.

* Paraphrase the major points of this chapter in the space provided. What sticks out to you today in light of this week's theme of unwavering faith?

* What is God telling you about Himself in these verses?

* What is God telling you about yourself and/or others in this chapter of James?

* What steps will you take today in response to what God has revealed to you through His Word today? List at least two below.

What you need most

Your parents divorced. You find out you have cancer. You are the target of a mean girl at school. Someone started a rumor about you and your boyfriend. Your best friend moves across the country. You get cut from the team. Your mom loses her job.

Tough situations, aren't they? What do you need in all of these situations? What will help you in every one of them?

Jot down your answers here:

Your answers could be as different as the girls who are doing this Bible study. You probably wrote things like *prayer* or *someone to talk to*. You might have even written *a miracle*. All of those would be helpful. But James offers one other thing that is essential for triumphing over trials.

Read James 1:5-8.

⁎ What does James focus on in these verses? Write your answer here:

⁎ How would you define

_____?

⁎ Now, answer that question in the space provided.

Why do all of these situations need wisdom? Because wisdom is the ability to apply what you know about a spiritual truth. And when you face a trial—something that tests your strength, patience, endurance, and stick-to-itiveness—applying truth to your current situation is **critical**.

And the only place to find wisdom is the Only Wise One.

✱ WISDOM'S SOURCE

Why can't you rely on your own wisdom? Why do you need the wisdom of God? Those are good—but difficult—questions. So, what does the Bible say about human wisdom?

Check out 1 Corinthians 1:25 to find out.

⁎ What did you learn?

We need wisdom in the midst of trials. And thankfully, God offers a way to for us to receive it.

Reread James 1:5 to find out how to get wisdom.

⁎ According to this verse, who is able to receive wisdom?

* How does God offer wisdom?

* Why does that matter?

Notice that James said, "If any of you lacks wisdom." He didn't say that wisdom was just for the super-spiritual or the mega-holy. He doesn't keep it on reserve just for your youth minister, pastor, parents, Sunday School teacher, or Billy Graham. He said that you— even as a teen—can have wisdom. Not only that, but God will give it freely and generously. He will give it to you without making you feel like a loser. He won't rebuke you or insult you, and He doesn't just give wisdom to the people that are always at church or seem to have it all together. He wants to give you wisdom, and He wants you to have as much as you need.

But there's a catch.

✳ THE CONDITIONAL PROMISE

According to James, there's a condition attached to this promise, an "if you will, then I will…"

Read James 1:6-8 to find out that condition.

* What is it?

* What illustration does James use to describe a person who doesn't have faith? Why is that a good illustration?

* Is doubt a sin? Why or why not?

* How is a person who doubts described in verse 8? What does it mean to be "indecisive" and "unstable"?

WEEK 2

* Think about your journey of faith. When could you describe your faith as being indecisive or unstable?

These verses have always confused me. In the middle of my tough times, sometimes I doubt. I wonder where God is, and I question His goodness. Is that wrong? What was James trying to tell us in these verses? To answer that, let's look at the words James originally used when he wrote his letter.

Read over the definitions below.

believe: be firmly persuaded and convinced

doubt: be divided in his mind; to hesitate or to waver

double-minded: trying to embrace the way of God and the way of sin at the same time

unstable: restless, not firmly anchored, unsteady

Now, look at the activity at the top of the next column. In the spaces provided, write in the original definitions of the words that you just read. When you're done, read over the passage again, letting the definitions provide a little more depth.

"But when he asks, he must _____ _____ and not _____, because he who _____ is like a wave of the sea, blown and tossed by the wind. That man should not think he will receive anything from the Lord; he is a _____ man, _____ in all he does" (vv. 6-8, NIV)

* Based on these definitions, what was James trying to say in these verses? And what does it mean for you?

When you examine what the words actually mean, you get a clearer picture of what James was trying to say. When you ask for God's wisdom to help you through troubles, you need to be firm in your conviction of God, His grace, and your assurance of His trustworthiness. When you go back and forth between belief and disbelief in God—those moments when you trust one minute and doubt the next—you're like a ship tossed around in a storm. You're not firmly anchored in God. You're trying to embrace both what God offers and what the world offers. You are divided, double-minded, and restless. And when you are restless, you can't gain God's wisdom.

It's not that God is holding out on you or taunting you. He would gladly give you wisdom (remember, He gives generously and freely) if you would stop running everywhere else in the world to find a solution instead of humbling yourself before Him and admitting that you need His help.

When you face a situation that you can't conquer (and there will be many of those in your life), you have a choice: you can believe in God and His ways, or you can try to figure it out on your own. You can't embrace your ways and God's ways at the same time (being double-minded). Only when you are anchored in God (not unstable) and humbly admit that you need His direction, can you receive the wisdom you desperately need.

We spend a majority of our faith journeys like a wave in the ocean tossed by the wind. But it doesn't have to be that way. Decide now to believe in God no matter what the circumstances. Resolve to trust Him no matter what life throws your way. Choose to believe that God is who He says He is, that His ways are better than yours, and that He will give you what you need to endure this current trial. You will have doubts in your journey of faith, and when you let those doubts shape the foundation of your faith, it becomes unsteady. But when your faith is rooted in God and His trustworthiness, it can't be shaken.

This passage reminds me of a story in the Gospels. You should be fairly familiar with it.

Read Matthew 14:22-31 and complete the paraphrase of the story in the next column. As you read, jot down any notes or verses that stick out to you below.

Jesus made the disciples _____
_____. After dismissing the
crowds, Jesus _____. When
the evening came, _____.
The boat was already over a mile from the shore,
_____ because _____.
_____ Around three in
the morning, Jesus decided to _____
_____. The disciples
saw him and _____. In
response to their fear, Jesus _____
_____. Of all of the
disciples in the boat, _____
was the only one to say anything to Jesus. He asked
_____. Jesus told him to
_____. And everything
was going great until
_____, and then Peter
cried out, _____! Jesus said
_____ and reached out to
grab Peter's hand.

I sometimes wonder if James thought about this encounter between Jesus and Peter when he wrote his letter. I don't know that he did, but he could have. In that passage from Matthew, all of the disciples were in the same storm. But only Peter trusted Jesus enough to step out of the boat and onto the water's surface. Peter was fine until he stopped looking to Jesus and started looking at his surroundings. The storm was still there. But in an instant, Peter's focus was split. He was double-minded—fearful of the storm, yet trying to believe in Jesus at the same time.

But the story doesn't end there.

Read Matthew 14:31-33 and fill in the rest of the story below.

When Jesus caught Peter, he _____
_____. Then, the two
of them got into the boat and _____.
Then the others in the boat _____
_____ and said _____
_____.

I used to think that Jesus was chastising Peter for his swan dive into the waves. But then I noticed that Jesus called Peter "you of little faith." Notice Jesus didn't say, "you of no faith." A little faith is better than no faith at all. It's only my opinion, but I think the question, "Why did you doubt?," was meant to help Peter process the experience. I think Jesus was helping Peter to see that he could have trusted Jesus the entire way back to the boat.

✱ WHERE ARE YOU?

In this story, the disciples and Peter represent different levels of faith and trust in the middle of a storm. Absolute faith, doubt, trust, fear, and everything in between are on full display in this story.

Think about a situation in your own life—a storm called _____ *(algebra or cancer or frenemies or grief or whatever. . .)* In the middle of that storm, you are just like one of the characters in the story you just studied. Whom are you most like? Peter before he walked on water? As he walked? When he was sinking? Or are you more like one of the disciples who stayed in the boat?

Describe that storm in your life. Record the name of the character in the story you're most like right now and jot down your reasons for choosing that character.

The good news is that Jesus takes you just as you are, wherever you are on your journey of faith. The even better news is that He loves you too much to leave you there. He longs to give you the wisdom to endure the trial and move forward, but you must believe and trust that He is bigger and stronger than whatever you face. You must trust Him enough to ask Him for the help you desperately need.

TRAINING MANUAL

Today, you'll read James 2. Use the following outline to help guide your interaction with Scripture as the Holy Spirit speaks to you.

✳ Pray.

✳ Read the entire chapter.

✳ Paraphrase the major points of this chapter below. When you're done, compare this list to the one you compiled last week. What's different? How?

✳ What is God telling you about Himself in these verses?

✳ What is God telling you about yourself and/or others in this passage?

✳ What steps will you take today to let what you've read in this chapter of James change the way you live?

Keep your eye on the prize.

The last couple of days of study have been full of heavy (and sometimes difficult) truths to absorb. You've learned that you will face trials in your journey of faith, that joy comes later, and that doubt can keep you from gaining God's wisdom. After all of that heavy stuff, you might be asking yourself if there's any good news in this Bible study.

Absolutely!

Read James 1:9-12 and summarize what it says. Think about how these verses apply to trials. Write your thoughts here:

You might be wondering if James needed an energy drink because in these verses, he seems to go off on a tangent, unable to concentrate or keep his thoughts focused. In one sentence (v. 8), he's talking about an unstable, indecisive man; in the next, he's talking about a rich man and poor man. What's the connection? Was James just rambling? Let's investigate.

Go back to page 18 and recall to whom this letter was written.

✷ Who was James writing this letter to? What was their situation?

Most of the people whom James was addressing in this letter were displaced Jews. They'd been conquered by a foreign king and shipped off to some foreign land, so they didn't exactly have time to sell their chariots, pack up their mules, and gather all their cherished belongings. They had simply grabbed what they could carry and left—and a lot of treasured belongings likely got left behind.

So maybe that sheds some light on James' discussion of the poor man in James 1:9-12. The people he was writing to didn't have a lot of stuff. They didn't have much money. But what does all that talk about rich people have to do with anything?

To figure that out, you have to know that the Jews believed that God showed favor on people by blessing them financially. In their minds, wealth equaled godliness, meaning the more godly you were, the richer God made you. Therefore, the poorest of the poor were generally considered to be the least godly people. (It doesn't work that way, FYI.) So in James 1:9-12, James was taking that idea on, reminding his readers, wealthy and poor alike, that having a lot of stuff doesn't mean much. Material stuff is temporary—one quick gust, and it's all gone.

I think what James wanted his readers to walk away with was an understanding that everyone goes through trials. No one gets a free pass from tough times. And having a lot of stuff doesn't mean you're anymore godly than anyone else or somehow immune to facing tough times.

By now, James' readers were probably wondering—just like you are—what the purpose of life's trials was. If trials don't exist to show God's judgment or blessing, then why do we have to face them? James tells us in verse 12.

Read James 1:12.

✳ What point does James make? Use your imagination and draw it below.

✳ THE CROWN

God promises a crown of life to us when we have passed the test and endured life's trials. When I first read this verse, I'll admit I wasn't that excited about the crown thing. I thought to myself, *A crown? Really? That's it? That's the reward for enduring life's toughest challenges?* I'm not a girly-girl, so the thought of getting a tiara just didn't encourage me. There had to be more to this than a simple piece of metal, or James wouldn't have made such a big deal out of it. So I did a little digging, and what I found made this verse come to life for me.

In ancient times, when people heard the word *crown*, they would have pictured one of four kinds of crowns:

Crown of flowers: This crown would have been worn at festivals, feasts, weddings, and times of joy.

Crown of royalty: This crown would have been worn by the members of the royal family and others in positions of authority.

Crown of victory: This crown would have been given to the winner in an athletic game.

Crown of honor: This crown signified some sort of honor or dignity that had been bestowed on a person.[1]

So why does that matter to you? You don't exactly get a crown for winning the 4x400 relay at a track meet. And you're not exactly royalty. Just stay with me.

Below are four Scripture verses. Next to each, write the name of the crown (from the list you just read) that best matches the topic of the verses.

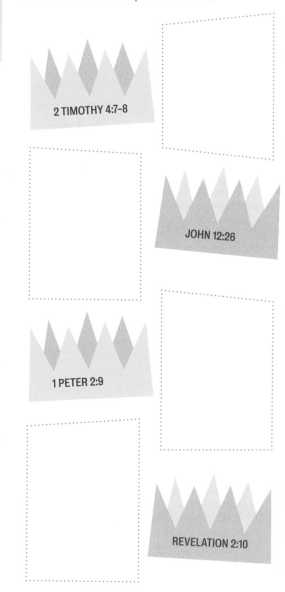

2 TIMOTHY 4:7–8

JOHN 12:26

1 PETER 2:9

REVELATION 2:10

James' use of the phrase "crown of life" is no typo. In fact, it could be better translated as "the crown which consists of life."[2] Real life is only found in a relationship with God. When we become Christians, we become part of a priesthood, royalty even. We are bestowed with honor and dignity. We will be victors (because Jesus was the victor). And one day, we will be participants in the wedding feast in heaven. Frankly speaking, that's one reception I don't want to miss.

The crown was simply a visual picture for James' readers. These early Christians were not in the best of situations and needed to know that persevering—sticking with the life of faith in Jesus Christ—is worth it. James used an item, the crown, that most people could relate to in order to make his point: A life with God—even in the midst of suffering and persecution—is more valuable and full of more life than any life without God, even if it's filled with comfort and ease.

✳ IN YOUR OWN WORDS

Imagine for a moment that a teacher at school is giving you a rough time for your faith in Jesus. She teaches science and constantly makes fun of people (especially you) who believe in God. Sometimes, she just makes snide remarks. Other times, she's rude and uncaring, and her words wound. But every time she acts that way, you simply answer her with gentleness and respect, explaining why you believe the way you do.

After class one day, a friend walks up to you and says, "I don't know why you keep putting up with that. And I don't understand why you keep believing in this God stuff. Is it worth all this harassment? Why don't you just give up?"

✳ What would you say? James gave his reasons in today's Scripture passage. Now it's your turn to give yours. Explain your reasons in the space provided.

✳ AND IF YOU NEEDED MORE ENCOURAGEMENT

Verse 12 is meant to be pure encouragement for believers (for us and James' original audience). If the message in this verse isn't enough to keep you going, you can even be encouraged by the very words themselves. Let me show you.

✳ Read the verse again, maybe even in a couple of different translations to help you understand it a little better. Then in the space below, write down any words that have a positive message in them. Next to each word, write down why it is encouraging, helpful, or uplifting. This will require a little more thought, so take your time.

I am a word geek. In school, I loved diagramming sentences. Even now, I love looking up Bible words in the original Greek and dissecting what they mean. I love pondering Scripture. It's like letting tomato sauce simmer. The longer you let it mull in your brain, the richer the meaning, flavor, and depth of your understanding.

This verse is rich in flavor, meaning, and depth. First, notice that James calls the person who endures trials "blessed." That's not the term I would use to describe a person going through a trial. So why does he use that word? Because James understood that even in the pain, God's plan and God's purposes prevail (Rom. 8:28).

James also used another little term that carries a big punch. It's the tiny word "when." He didn't say, "*If* he passes the test" in verse 12; he said, "*When* he passes the test." I love that assurance.

And did you notice the word "will"? That's a strong word, not like a wimpy *might, could* or *possibly*. It's definite. We **will** receive the crown of life. Definitely. It's a guarantee. Why? Because God promised it.

And He doesn't break His promises.

✱ WHAT HAPPENS TO YOUR CROWN?

Scripture doesn't tell us much about the crown of life we will receive. There is no description of its shape, size, color, or composition. There is no verse that tells us if we will wear them in heaven or even if each person's crown looks different based on our trials on earth. But Scripture does give us a little hint of what we might eventually do with our crowns.

Read Revelation 4:1-11.

✳ What is described here?

✳ Which description stands out most in your mind? Why?

✳ Whose throne is described in this passage?

✳ Who is described in verse 10?

✳ What do the elders do before the "One seated on the throne"? Why?

What a picture! It's hard to wrap my mind around what it will be like to stand before God while He's seated on His throne. I think that's why John used the language he did in the passage from Revelation that you just read. He was just grasping for words, words that couldn't do justice to what he had seen. I may not be able to picture what it's like to stand before God, but I can tell you what I'm going to do. I am going to fall on my face and do exactly what the elders did. I will worship "the One who lives forever and ever." And just like the elders, I will cast my crown at His feet.

I can think of no other response that would be worthy of who He is.

1. William Barclay, *The Letters of James and Peter* (Louisville, Ky.: Westminster John Knox Press, 2003), 55-56.

2. Ibid, 56.

TRAINING MANUAL

Today, you'll read James 3. Use the following outline to help guide your interaction with Scripture as the Holy Spirit speaks to you.

* Pray.

* Read the entire chapter.

* What is God telling you about Himself in this passage?

* Paraphrase the major points of this chapter. Read the passage in light of what you've been studying this week. Notice anything different from last week?

* What is God telling you about yourself and/or others in these verses?

* What steps will you take today to respond to the truths God has revealed to you in James 3?

What's in a word?

One outcome of the birth of social media is that every person can be a writer. In the time it takes to watch an episode of "Glee," you can set up your own blog. And blogs are everywhere. In fact, the Wall Street Journal reported in 2009 that in the United States alone, 20 million people are bloggers.[1] The problem is that not all of those self-proclaimed writers have a good grasp of grammar, vocabulary, or the basic mechanics that make up good writing—which has led to some really bad online text. And one of the biggest mistakes people often make is using a word in an incorrect context.

Think you're a pro in vocabulary? Let's test your knowledge. Complete the quiz below by matching the correct word with its definition.

Irritate	to receive with approval
Aggravate	to create a negative condition
Accept	person with highest rank or main participant
Except	to improve or complete something
Principle	a statehouse
Principal	to increase the severity of an existing negative condition
Complement	more distant
Compliment	praise or flattery
Imply	to express indirectly
Infer	more time or quantity
Farther	to conclude from evidence
Further	excluding; other than
Capital	city at the center of politics or industry; wealth in business
Capitol	a standard or rule that often pertains to morality or nature

In today's Bible study, we'll take an in-depth look at two words that are often used interchangeably. When it comes to surviving the hard times, being able to distinguish between the two words can make all the difference. You're about to see why.

✳ A LITTLE REVIEW

Before we go any further in our study of James, we need to do a little review. Look back at the pages from this week to help you answer the following questions.

✳ On page 47, you learned that trials are _____.
Everybody will experience them in life.

✳ On page 49, you learned that when (not if!) you face a trial, God will give you the _____ you need to endure that trial.

✳ On page 43, you learned that when you ask for wisdom, you need to _____ that God will provide for you.

✳ On page 48, you learned that you will receive a _____ for enduring through trials.

✳ On page 48, you learned that

_____
—sticking with a life of faith in Jesus Christ—is worth it.

Today's study continues with the theme of enduring trials. It will focus on how to distinguish between trials and temptations, who's responsible for them, and how to respond.

✳ YOU MADE ME DO IT!

Read James 1:13-15, then consider the questions in the next column.

What is the end result of sin?

If that is the case, why do you think so many people continue to sin?

What do these verses say God does NOT do?

Why would a girl say God was tempting her?

What do these verses teach you about God's character?

According to these verses, what is the source of temptation?

What tendency was James telling his readers to avoid in these verses?

What is the progression of sin? (Hint: 3 steps)

BONUS: What two fishing-related words are used?

Here are the answers. Check to see how you did:

What is the end result of sin? Death.

If that is the case, why do you think so many people continue to sin? Focus too much on immediate gratification; blinded by sin; sin is fun for a while; nobody told them

What do these verses say God does NOT do? Tempt anyone

Why would a girl say God was tempting her? To avoid taking responsibility for her actions

What do these verses teach you about God's character? He is holy—and cannot be tempted by sin. Can you imagine not being able to be tempted?

According to these verses, what is the source of temptation? Our own sinful desires; in other words, you are responsible for your own sin. That's painful to admit sometimes, but it's true!

What tendency was James telling his readers to avoid in these verses? To say that God is tempting them

What is the progression of sin? 3 steps: desire gives birth to sin; sin gives birth to death

BONUS: What two fishing-related words are used? Drawn away and enticed; the word "drawn" is like luring a fish out of its hiding place; enticed is the idea of putting a juicy worm on a hook.

✳ BREAK IT DOWN

From the beginning of creation, humanity has been playing the blame game. Adam blamed Eve; she blamed the serpent. We as human beings are good at trying to shift personal responsibility from ourselves to someone else. *My friends made me do it. I acted that way because she started a rumor about me. If I didn't dress this way, I'd lose my boyfriend. I listen to that music because there's nothing else that I like.* But James 1:13-15 makes it very clear that we sin because of our own sinful desires. When we give in to those desires (which is a choice), sin results. You are responsible for your choice. You are responsible for your own sin. And unfortunately, you bear the consequences of those sinful choices—and sometimes, so do others.

✳ NOT THE SAME, BUT CLOSE

It seems a little odd that all of the sudden, James started talking about temptation and sin. I mean, why? He had been talking about trials throughout the whole chapter. And we know that it's not a sin to go through a trial, so what's the connection? **Here it is:** while trials are not temptations from God, you **will be tempted** to sin in the midst of trials.

Here's an example: One of your classmates posts something mean about you on Facebook. In retaliation, you do the same thing and post something awful about her on your Facebook wall, talking about what a skank she is.

The first situation—her saying something awful about you on Facebook—was a trial. The second situation—when you responded by posting your own nasty note about her on your wall—was a temptation that became sin. You wanted to get back at her, and you saw the opportunity *(temptation)*, then you acted on it *(sin)* by posting about her on Facebook. See the difference? The two are not the same, but they are very much related. Trials and temptations are not from the same family, but they hang out with each other just the same.

Almost every trial you face will come with a temptation to sin. With God's help, you can recognize those areas of temptation and avoid the sin that would make the trial even worse.

✳ Listed below are some trials. Next to each, list some possible temptations you might face as you deal with the ordeal.

TRIAL	POSSIBLE TEMPTATIONS
Your boyfriend dumps you for another girl.	
Someone sends you a "sext."	
You get cut from the team.	
Your parents decide to divorce.	
You're forced to move to another state.	
A friend brings her parents' prescription drugs to camp.	
You make a horrible grade on your test.	
Your mom is diagnosed with cancer.	
The most popular girl at school starts a rumor about you.	
A friend dies in a wreck.	

See how easily you can be enticed into sin in the midst of a trial? Trials by nature test us—emotionally, physically, and spiritually. And if you are weary, frustrated, angry, scared, or sad, be on your guard. That's a prime time for the Enemy (the roaring lion who wants to devour you according to 1 Peter 5:8; more on him later) to bring out every trick in the book.

✳ To summarize your time in the Word today, take a moment to reflect on any trials you've faced recently. Ask yourself, *Did I sin while I was going through it?* If so, write a prayer to the Lord, asking Him to forgive you. If you're facing a trial right now, write a prayer to the Lord, asking Him to help you to not be snagged or pulled away by temptation.

One more day to go this week, sisters! You are doing great work!

1. Mark Penn and E. Kinney Zalesne, "America's Newest Profession: Bloggers for Hire," *Wall Street Journal* [online], 21 April 2009 [cited 11 July 2011]. Available from the Internet: *http://online.wsj.com/article/SB124026415808636575.html*

TRAINING MANUAL

WEEK

2

Today, you'll read James 4. Use the following outline to help guide your interaction with Scripture as the Holy Spirit speaks to you.

* Pray.

* Read the entire chapter.

* Paraphrase the major points of this chapter. Turn back to page 28 and compare this week's findings to last week's.

* What did God tell you about Himself in this passage?

* What is God telling you about yourself and/or others in these verses?

* What steps will you take to respond to what God has told you to do?

✳ *Good gifts from a loving Father*

What is God like? How would you describe His character? Why?

✳ In the area provided for you below, create a thought cloud that focuses on different character traits of God. Don't limit yourself. And be honest—there are no right or wrong answers. Just write down every trait of God that you can think of. If one trait is similar to another, just link them together with a line.

✳ INTRODUCING THE FATHER OF LIGHTS

Before we dig into the character of God, let's do a little more reviewing. (Gotta make sure you remember what you've learned this week!)

✳ In the space provided below, summarize the work you've done over the past four days. (You can look on page 53 for days 1-3, then add your notes about what you learned yesterday.)

GOD

Yesterday, you learned about trials and temptations, the source of both, and how one can lead to the other. Today's study will wrap up this week's focus on trials and the Christian life.

✳ Read James 1:16-18. These verses tell us a lot about the character of God. Create another thought cloud, but use these verses to make your cloud.

BIG
POWERFUL

GOD

Today's Bible study will focus on a certain aspect of God's character and why that trait would be important for the people who received James' letter—and to you!

✳ GOD AS GOOD

The first thing you learned about God in James 1:16-18 is that He is the generous Giver of perfect gifts. In other words, "Every good and perfect gift is from above" (v. 17, NIV). In that one verse, we learn that God loves to give to us—generously. And His gifts are good, because God is good. (Check out Ps. 119:68 for more on that.)

So what exactly does the fact that God is the good and generous Giver have to do with trials and temptations? A lot actually.

A good God doesn't bring temptation. (Remember? See vv. 13-15 for a reminder.) We can look at a situation and know that if it involves a temptation to do something wrong, it's not from God. Ever. God will not contradict His character (which is holy) or His Word (which says that God is not the author of temptation).

If you're facing a situation and you're not sure what to do, the first question you should ask is simply, *Will this lead to sin?* If it would lead to disobeying God—like lying to your parents to go out with a guy you like—then you know it's not from God. (Even if that guy is a Christian, and even if he's a great guy.)

The fact that God is good matters when you are in the fires of a trial. When you're in the middle of a nasty trial, you will be tempted to question God's goodness. Believe me, I've been there. You'll say things like, "If God was good, He wouldn't do this to me." Or, "If God really loved me, then this wouldn't be happening. And here's a classic: "If God is good, then why does bad stuff happen?" **Never allow your circumstances to define the character of God.** Situations change. God's character does not.

✳ What trials are you facing? How can the fact that God is good, even when the situations or your emotions don't seem to show God's goodness, help you in the middle of that trial? List a few of them and your thoughts below.

✳ GOD AS UNCHANGING

The second thing you learned about God in James 1:16-18 is that He is constant, consistent, and dependable. James calls Him the "Father of lights" in verse 17. In the original language, the word "lights" refers to the sun, moon, stars, and other stellar bodies up in the sky. And "Father" in this instance carries the idea of God as the "creator, preserver, governor of all men and things, watching over them with paternal love and care."

Put them together and you get what? God is the Creator and Preserver of the sun, moon, stars, and everything else there is. He's the Creator of everything, but He doesn't change like the things He has created.

Did you know that stars move? And so do the sun and the moon. Everything is in a constant state of change—your hair, your friends, the clouds in the sky, the caterpillar on the tree outside your window. Everything, that is, except God. James tells us that "with Him there is no variation or shadow by turning" (v. 17). In other words, "There is nothing deceitful in God, nothing two-faced, nothing fickle" (v. 17, *The Message*).

Think through the following questions.

✳ Why would it matter to people going through trials that God is constant and consistent?

✳ What difference does God's unchanging presence make in your own life? Why does it matter?

✳ GOD AS MERCIFUL

The third thing you should have learned about God in these verses? That God is merciful and gracious.

> ✳ Reread James 1:18. Why does this verse point to the mercy and grace of God?

The fact that God chose us, that He gave us a new birth through the death and resurrection of Jesus Christ, is a statement about His mercy and His grace. We don't deserve forgiveness, but He offers it. We don't deserve eternal life with Him, but He made it possible. He chose to give it to us.

> ✳ Why does the mercy and grace of God matter to people who are in the midst of a trial?

Because of God's grace and mercy, we have access to God. No matter what is going on in our lives, God promises that nothing can separate us from the love of God (Rom. 8:38-39) and that He will work all things together for the good of those who love Him (Rom. 8:28). Those verses are true. And they're true for you! Knowing those two truths can strengthen, encourage, and keep you going when you're struggling. You are never alone—and your trial is not useless.

✳ ONE MORE THOUGHT

> ✳ The last character trait of God from these verses is actually in verse 16. Look closely. What character trait can you find?

What does James call his readers in this verse? "Dearly loved brothers." Dearly loved by whom? Yes, James loved the church at Jerusalem—but more importantly, those people were dearly loved by God. Notice that James didn't say *brothers that God merely puts up with* or *people who drive God crazy with their unfaithfulness and sin.* James didn't call them a bunch of sinners who were a disappointment to God and unworthy of His love. He called them "dearly loved."

Of all the character traits that matter, this is the biggest: God is loving. He loves you furiously and without condition—even when you rebel against Him in huge ways. He yearns for a relationship with you (Jer. 31:20). You are the apple of His eye, the object of His holy affection, the one for whom He was willing to die.

You may be reading this in disbelief. No one has ever loved you unconditionally. In fact, you may have been the object of fierce violation by others through abuse or betrayal of some sort. The idea that love could be real and true, pure and holy, good and free, and perfect and healing is just beyond your realm of possibility. **But there is a God who loves you**—purely, freely, perfectly. His love is real. It is good, and it heals. His love is the one thing you can count on in this life and in the next. No matter what you have done—or what has been done to you—you can fall safely into the arms of a God who promises that you can rest securely in Him (Deut. 33:12). Having a safe, secure place to fall makes all the difference in the world. And it can make all the difference in your heart. Thank you, God!

TRAINING MANUAL

Today, you'll read James 5. Use the following outline to help guide your interaction with Scripture as the Holy Spirit speaks to you.

WEEK
2

* Pray.

* Read the entire chapter.

* Paraphrase the major points of this chapter. How are they different from what you wrote last week? (See page 38)

* What did God tell you about Himself in these verses?

* What is God telling you about yourself and/or others in James 5?

* How will you respond to what He has said to you?

week three

RESPONSIVE

Faith Under Pressure: Responsive

You walk by a store window and notice that your skirt is caught up in your panties.

You're eating with a friend and she says, "You've got a piece of something stuck in your teeth."

Looking into the lenses of a friend's glasses, you see a piece of your hair sticking straight up.

The reflection of a window. Seeing something from a friend's perspective. Seeing in a mirror. A reflected image on sunglasses. Besides being a little awkward, what do each of these situations have in common?

Answer: they all involve looking at a reflection. And what would you do in each of these situations? You would act on what you saw in your reflection.

Not acting would be stupid. You wouldn't knowingly walk around the mall with your hair sticking up, spinach in your teeth, or a definite wardrobe malfunction. It just wouldn't happen. You would instantly act on what you saw in your reflection.

This week will focus on faith that is **responsive**—faith that sees, then acts.

Hearing and doing

Read James 1:22-25. Based on these verses, complete the thoughts below.

Be _____ of the word and not just

_____.

When you don't do anything with what you have heard (or read) in the Word, you are _____ yourself. Why would James use that word? Explain.

According to this passage, a person who hears but doesn't act on what she hears is like what?

How are Christians supposed to look at God's Word?

_____

What does that mean?

James called Scripture

_____

According to these verses, what happens when you hear AND do what God's Word says?

What happens if you just take in God's Word and don't do anything with it?

James makes his point clear: hearing without doing is fruitless. In fact, he says that the person who just reads God's Word without doing what it says is deceiving herself. That's a pretty strong statement. Why would James say something like that?

✳ BAMBOOZLED

The word *deceive* can also mean *mislead*, *trick*, or *fool*. The person who just hears God's Word without acting on it is being misled or fooled. But how? She misleads herself by thinking less of Scripture than what it is—the God-breathed, authoritative, sacred word to humanity. A person like that believes one (or more) of the following myths about Scripture:

1. God's Word is relative and not absolute.
Those who believe this lie think that God's standards as laid out in Scripture are just an alternative way of living. You can pick and choose from what Scripture says to suit your needs. Everyone gets to pick which portions—if any!—of Scripture are meant for them to follow. Such a false idea probably sounds like this in your world: "You can believe in the Bible. I just don't. If it works for you, that's fine. But don't make me believe it, too." Or, you may hear something like "I believe in the Bible. But I also believe in the Book of Mormon."

WEEK 3

2. God's Word is a good luck charm.

Some girls think that if you carry your Bible to school, you'll have a good day. Others think that if you read your Bible before your physics exam, God will bless you for your effort. People who believe this lie might carry a Bible in their cars just in case.

3. God's Word will make you feel better.

If you are caught in this lie, you just read the portions of Scripture that make you feel good—like Psalm 23—and forget the rest. Things you might hear a person who's bought into this lie say include: "The Old Testament? It's too hard to understand. And besides, all that stuff in the Bible about war and judgment just makes me feel guilty. God doesn't want me to feel that way."

4. God's Word is a tool for debate.

If you've ever spouted off Scripture at the lunch table just to make your point in an argument, then you're guilty of this myth. People who believe this lie about Scripture simply think it's a tool to use to get their own way. If you're trapped in this lie, you might find a verse to prove to your parents that they should let you do something. Get the point? It's all about winning in an intellectual battle of the minds and using Scripture to do so.

At the heart of the matter is one truth: we cannot just soak in the Truth and not allow it to affect our lives—our words and actions. God didn't send His Word merely to make us feel better, give us options for reading, or to win an argument in debate class. He wants to tell us something. And most of the time, what He tells us in Scripture requires a response.

What's really scary is that some people go their entire lives believing those myths. Because they never take it to heart and act on it, they never choose to repent of their sin and confess their need for a Savior. They live without hope in this life—and the next.

* KEEP LOOKING

There's a truth in our world that is undisputable: if you don't eat, you die. If an elephant doesn't eat hay, grass, and other grains, it dies. If mosquitoes don't suck the blood of animals (and people), they die. If plants don't do their photosynthesis thing, they turn brown and die. All living things must continually feed on the things that give them the nutrients they need to survive.

Reread verse 25. There's a word in this verse that reminds us that we must continually feed on God's Word. What is it?

Notice the word *perseveres.* Other translations use the word *continues* or phrases such as *sticks with it* in verse 25. In other words (no pun intended), you can't just read the Bible once. If you persevere in reading it, you continually look into God's Word and live out the truths that you find there. If you don't, your spiritual growth will stall—or just die out. Jesus talked about this principle in the Gospel of John.

Read John 15:5-6. Draw two pictures based on what you read:

  ⁎ Remaining

  ⁎ Not Remaining

How do we remain in Jesus? By reading His Word. Remember, He is the Word made flesh. Everything He said and did communicates something from God the Father that we need to hear—and act on.

⁑ PERFECT LAW OF FREEDOM

Look at verse 25 again. You'll see that James also called God's Word "the perfect law of freedom." Putting the words *law* and *freedom* in the same sentence seems ironic, like putting the words *blessed* and *trials* in the same sentence. (See page 49 if you don't remember what I'm talking about.)

  ⁎ So, how can a law bring freedom?

Laws are actually meant for our good. Not killing another person frees us of the emotional, social, and physical consequences that occur when you take a life. Slowing down in a school zone protects children (and you!) who are walking home from school. Remaining drug-free frees you from the pain of addiction, the social stigma of being a user, and the physical destruction that occurs to the body (among other things).

The same applies for God's law which is made perfect or complete in Jesus. When we follow His example, we conform ourselves to His image (Rom. 8:29), the image of the One we were created to be like (Gen. 1:27). When you become more like Jesus, you become more like "you"—the person God dreamed of when He created you, the person He created you to be—with all of your unique traits, individual likes and dislikes, strength of character, and loving nature.

And being yourself is freedom. Real freedom.

TRAINING MANUAL

WEEK
3

Today, you'll read James 1 in its entirety for the third time. Use the following outline to help guide your interaction with Scripture as the Holy Spirit speaks to you.

* Pray.

* Read the entire chapter.

* Paraphrase the major points of this chapter:

* What is God telling you about Himself in these verses? Did anything different stick out to you in light of the past few weeks' study?

* What is God telling you about yourself and/or others in James 1?

* What has God said to you through this chapter of Scripture? What steps will you take to respond?

Let the Word take root.

You're sitting in class, bored out of your mind. Well, actually, your mind is wandering. Your science teacher is explaining how to balance equations, but you're distracted by the beautiful skies, bright sunshine, and the guys' P.E. class that is running on the track a short distance outside your window. In your daydreaming, you hear your teacher say five words that snap you back to reality: *you might see this again.*

Translation: whatever your teacher is talking about will be on an upcoming test. Those five words are teacher-code for *pay attention—this is important!*

✳ HEADS UP

Today's passage, James 1:19-20, begins with the same sort of warning. James was telling his church (and us) to pay attention to what he was about to say because he thought it was pretty important.

Read James 1:19-20. In the warning sign below, write down James' warning. What was he telling his readers to do?

Just like the teacher told you to pay attention to what he was saying because he knew that there was a huge test looming on the horizon, James also explained why he wanted his readers to follow his instruction.

Reread James 1:19-20 to discover the reason he told us to keep our anger in check. Summarize his reasons in the space provided:

James knew that nothing good happens when we let anger get the best of us. Unchecked anger results in heated words that can cause severe and painful damage. In this instance, the word "righteousness" carries the idea of what is right or what brings justice. When you and I are quick to get angry, we decide that the other person is wrong, guilty, or at fault, which often leads us to treat that person in a way that isn't right or fair.

...

WEEK 3

* Think about a time recently when you got angry over something and didn't treat someone with respect, kindness, or fairness—only to find out later that you were the one at fault. You got angry at the other person so quickly that you didn't stop to see the whole situation. Use the space below to tell your story.

Unfortunately, we're all guilty of losing our tempers and being slow to listen, quick to speak, and very quick to get mad. You're not alone. **Think about this:** would James have told his readers to pay attention to his words about anger if they were all really good at keeping their anger under control? Probably not.

✱ UMM . . . I'M CONFUSED

By now, you might be thinking to yourself, *This is great advice, but I'm confused. Yesterday we were talking about the importance of listening and acting on God's Word, and now we're talking about anger? I don't get the connection.*

Read James 1:21. Complete the thoughts below to get a clearer picture of why James was talking about anger.

What to get rid of:

_____

Reason to lose them:

_____

What to receive:

_____

Reason to receive it:

_____

Get the picture? God's Word makes the difference. In this verse, James described what it's like when God's Word doesn't take root in someone's life. He used words like "moral filth" and "evil excess." *The Message* describes a Word-less life as "spoiled virtue and cancerous evil" that should be thrown away like the trash. Any way you describe it, a life without God's Word isn't a pretty existence. In the passage you studied yesterday, James challenged you to hear and respond to God's Word. These verses explain why interacting with Scripture is so vitally important—life without it leads to evil.

...

* Think about the world you and I live in. What are some words you would use to describe it? Think about the moral climate, the things people chase after, and the way people treat each other. Write them in the space below.

You might be pretty discouraged, but there is hope, and it is found in verse 25. What can save you from this?

Write your answer in large letters on top of all the adjectives you listed above.

The Word saves us. It saves us like a man rescued from a fire, a girl air-lifted out of a flood, a woman healed of an incurable disease, or a child freed from kidnappers. The heart of the problem, though, isn't fire or flood or disease or a person. It is sin. **We are saved from sin.**

The word "saved" in this verse literally means to bring into the kingdom. How can the Word save us? Because in His Word we read about the birth, life, death, and resurrection of Christ and its significance in human history. Scripture tells us the story of redemption, the story of how you and I can be rescued, healed, and freed. James understood that the only solution for evil is holiness that comes from being in a right relationship with God through Jesus Christ.

✴ PUTTING 2 AND 2 TOGETHER

James 1:22 makes a lot more sense when you read verse 21 with it. The phrases of these two verses are scrambled below. **Put them back in the right order and rewrite the verses as James penned them so many years ago.**

Deceiving yourselves

Humbly receive the implanted word

But be doers of the word and not hearers only

Ridding yourselves of all moral filth and evil

Which is able to save you

Why is being a doer of the word important? Because unless the Word takes root in our lives and we act on it, we'll never be saved. We will be deceiving ourselves into thinking that we're OK without Christ, when the truth is that **He is everything.**

✻ DEEP ROOTS

James understood that it's not enough just to read the Bible like you read the morning newspaper or the latest book.

What word or phrase in verse 21 describes the place Scripture should have in your life?

God's Word needs to take root in our lives. It needs to find a humble (v. 21), receptive, willing, open heart. Maybe James was remembering one of Jesus' parables when he wrote this letter. Let's take a look.

Read Luke 8:4-8,11-15. In the space below, summarize Jesus' parable:

Jesus described four different soils representing a person's receptiveness to God's Word. To close your study today, take an inventory of your life.

✻ Which soil best represents your willingness to receive God's Word? Circle it. Then close your time praying. Ask God to make soft and receptive any hardened, rocky, thorny places in your heart.

A PATH-LIKE HEART

A ROCKY HEART

A THORN-INFESTED HEART

A GOOD (OPEN) HEART

TRAINING MANUAL

Today, you'll read James 2. Use the following outline to help guide your interaction with Scripture as the Holy Spirit speaks to you.

* Pray.

* Read the entire chapter.

* Paraphrase the major points of this chapter:

* What is God telling you about Himself in James 2?

* What is God telling you about yourself and/or others in this chapter? Did He show you something new this week? Explain.

* What steps will you take to respond to what God has shown you through your persevering study of His Word?

☀ Inside out

There's a story told about a tree that grew in the center of a small town. It was huge. Massive. Beautiful. Over the years, it had become the pride and joy of the town. Kids climbed onto its branches, families ate lunch under its shade, and visitors were given directions using the tree as a reference point.

Every fall, as the temperature dropped and the winds shifted to the north, the tree began to lose its leaves and settle in for the dormant winter months. It endured wind and rain, snow and sleet, and bone-chilling temperatures.

But one spring, just as the trees were beginning to bud again, a massive thunderstorm blew into town, complete with strong winds, lightning, and hail. Everyone huddled along the storefronts under the awnings to stay dry and safe. In the midst of this wild storm, they heard a massive crrrrack, followed by an even louder thud.

To the town's dismay, the sound they had heard was the destruction of the beloved tree. The strong winds had toppled the tree. It lay in the center of town, broken across its base. The people stood in shock. How could wind—even a strong wind—cause such a mighty tree to fall?

When they looked inside the tree, they found their answer. Unknown to them, just as the leaves were falling from the trees, a disease infiltrated the tree from the roots and continued spreading, straight into the heart of the tree itself. The outside still looked fine, but the core of the tree was dead.

That story relates to your interaction with God and His Word today. You'll be reading James 1:26-27, in which James will challenge you to examine your life to evaluate whether or not you are demonstrating a genuine walk with God, or just maintaining the outward appearance of godliness—like a tree that looks great on the outside but is diseased within.

✳ REVIEW

Over the last two days, you've discovered the importance of being in God's Word and allowing it to change the way you think and act. James talked about a life without God's Word (Jas. 1:19-21) as well as the benefits of being transformed. He repeats this pattern again in the last two verses, today's focal passage, comparing worthless religion with true religion, which is pure and undefiled.

✳ AGAIN?

James closes out the first portion of his letter (originally, it didn't have chapters and verses like the way you're reading it today) by going back to a subject he'd already covered.

Read James 1:26 to discover what topic he returned to. Write it down here:

Yep, another reminder that our speech tells us a lot about the true nature of our relationship with God.

  ✳ Just as a reminder, what did he mention earlier in verse 19?

* What is different about the description in verse 26?

* What is similar about the description in verse 26?

* What adjective did James use to describe the religion of a person whose tongue isn't under control?

* Why do you think James used the adjective "deceived" to describe a person who doesn't control her tongue but calls herself religious?

* Why do you think James brought up the subject of controlling your speech again?

Worthless. That's a strong word. Yet, that's how James described the religion of a person who didn't control her tongue. Earlier, James talked specifically about keeping your words in check when you're angry. In this round, James didn't get specific. He just challenged believers to control every aspect of their speech, not just when they got their feathers ruffled.

We don't know exactly why James returned to the topic of speech again in chapter 1, but we can surmise that it must have been an issue for the early Christians, because he talked about it again in later chapters. (We'll get there eventually.) While we don't know why the people of his time needed to hear this strong warning, we do know why people in our day need to hear it—why we need to hear it.

Think about a typical day in your life. Using the space provided, write down all the times, places, and situations in which you are tempted to unbridle your tongue and let the words fly:

Sharing the bathroom with your sister _____

_____

_____

Riding to school _____

_____

Hearing about last weekend's party _____

_____

_____

At your locker _____

_____

Eating lunch _____

_____

In class _____

_____

Texting your friends _____

_____

_____

Online at night _____

James wrote this warning to believers who lived before the invention of the telephone, before texting and social media were the primary means of communication. If those people needed a warning, then how much more do you and I need that reminder about our words now?

As painful as it is, we need to be reminded of this truth: we can't do all the outward stuff of religion (going to church, fasting, worship) without also showing signs of an inward change that results in controlled speech. In fact, James said that our religion is worthless if we can't control our speech. *Ouch!*

Just one other note about these verses: the word "tongue" in the original Greek was considered a feminine word (like words in Spanish or French that are either masculine or feminine). And what gender seems to have more difficulty in controlling speech? Yep, the girls. Just something to think about…

✱ PURE RELIGION

After reading James' description of worthless religion, you (like James' original readers) are probably wondering what real, true religion looks like. If so, James provided an answer that they would readily recognize. Keep in mind, though, that these are not the only signs of an authentic relationship with God. These are just examples.

Read James 1:27. What two signs of true religion did James highlight?

1. To

_____

2. To

_____

James gave two examples of authentic faith. One focuses our attention outward, while the other focuses inward.

"To look after" the orphans and widows was not an original concept for these Jewish Christians. In fact, they were very, very familiar with it.

Read Exodus 22:21-23 and jot down the commands given in these verses:

The Jews knew this command. It was a part of their heritage, their history, and their laws. In their culture, the orphans and the widows were the most needy people. They had no source of income, and no one to protect or provide for them. They were the most vulnerable. James described believers helping them "in their distress." The word *distressed* means, "crushed, pressed, or squeezed."[1] What James wanted his readers to understand was that these people felt the weight of being alone and vulnerable.

You may not come across widows or orphans very much in your school, church, or town. But every day, you come across people who are crushed, pressed, and squeezed by the storms of life. People who are very much alone and vulnerable.

 Who are they?

James made it clear—when you are receptive to God and His Word, your interactions with others will change. Your life will bear the mark of kindness, compassion, and mercy toward others.

* Look back over that list and think about the people you listed. How have you looked after them? Do you take care of them? Why or why not?

* INWARD CLEANLINESS

James wrote to the people that their outward lives should show true religion. So should the inward life.

Read James 1:27 again and find the command to the readers about their own hearts. Jot the instruction in the margin.

James challenged his readers to keep themselves "unstained by the world." The word "stained" was a reference to Old Testament sacrifices that could not contain any blemish or spot or defect—no lame leg, deformed back, and so forth. Obviously, we don't follow that sacrificial system now, so what does being "stained" mean?

James said not to be stained by the world. In other words, believers are to seek moral purity, a life that is free of the things the world values, like self-reliance, selfishness, greed, lust, power, and violence.

To close out your time with the Word today, evaluate your own life by looking at the list of things the world values in the previous paragraph. What worldly pursuits are staining your life right now? Circle them. Spend time in prayer, asking God to free you from the grip of those desires and to give you passion to pursue Him fully.

1. "thlipsis," *The Complete Word Study Dictionary: New Testament*, Spiros Zodhiates, ed. (Chatanooga, Tenn.: AMG Publishers, 1992), 736-737.

WEEK 3

DAY 3
TRAINING MANUAL

Today, you'll read James 3. Use the following outline to help guide your interaction with Scripture as the Holy Spirit speaks to you.

* Pray.

* Read the entire chapter.

* Paraphrase the major points of James 3.

* What is God telling you about Himself in this chapter? Notice any differences from last week's reading?

* What is God telling you about yourself and/or others in James 3?

* What has God said to you in these verses? What steps will you take in response?

Don't play favorites.

One of my favorite things to do when I have some down time is to work puzzles. I know it's pretty old-fashioned or lame. But I enjoy seeing how all of the individual pieces come together to create a bigger whole. Over the years, I've learned one important principle of puzzle-working: every once in a while, you need to look at the big picture to keep everything in perspective.

That same principle applies to in-depth Bible study. As you are studying God's Word, looking at where you've been and the overall theme can help you keep perspective when looking at the little pieces of Scripture.

Look back at the first three days of study you have completed this week. Summarize them by writing down three main themes, one for each day:

＊ 1.

＊ 2.

＊ 3.

Overall, this week focuses on faith that is receptive to God's Word. First, you learned about the importance of living out God's Word and not just reading

it. The second day emphasized what a life without God's Word looks like. Yesterday, you discovered some characteristics of life in the Word—the impact a pure and undefiled religion has both externally and internally.

If you recall from yesterday's session, James' example of taking care of the orphans and widows was one of many examples of faith that is receptive to God's Word. Taking care of these forgotten people is important, but it is not the only demonstration of true religion. James gave more examples in chapter 2—and it's time to dig into that Scripture!

✱ CAN'T HOLD ON TO BOTH

James' command to his readers (and to us) was short and simple, but easier said than done. **Read James 2:1 and summarize it below:**

＊ How would you define favoritism?

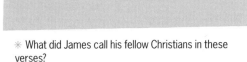

＊ What did James call his fellow Christians in these verses?

＊ Why might that particular nickname be important when talking about favoritism?

* Why shouldn't Christians show favoritism? Why does that matter?

James' command was pretty straightforward: don't show favoritism. In his mind, playing favorites was inconsistent with the Christian faith altogether. That may have been why he called his readers "brothers." He wanted them (and us) to understand that we're all in the same family with God as our Father, so nobody gets to be the favorite. Why?

Read the following Scripture passages. Then, at the space provided below, write what every one of them has in common:

* Deuteronomy 10:17-18

* Deuteronomy 16:18-20

* Luke 20:20-21

* Acts 10:34-35

We shouldn't show favoritism because God does not show favoritism. He doesn't treat us differently based on our race, gender, or economic status. And because we are bearers of His name, we are to bear His character as well.

✳ FOR EXAMPLE

Like all good pastors, James gave an example of favoritism to demonstrate what the church was **not** supposed to do.

* Read James 2:2-4 and summarize his example here:

* Put it in your own context. What would it look like for you (or one of your friends) to show a similar kind of favoritism at your church? Describe that scenario here:

Unfortunately, favoritism plays a role in your church—and in mine. If a shabby-looking guy was sitting in "my spot" in church, I might avoid him altogether, especially if my husband wasn't with me. I would avoid sitting beside him or behind him (so I didn't have to greet him during the welcome portion of our service). On the other hand, if a clean-shaven man dressed in a nice suit was sitting there, I might sit behind him. I would welcome him and shake his hand. It's painful for me to type this, but it's true.

It's probably true for you, too. We treat people differently based on outward appearances sometimes.

James said that when I do that, I've become a judge with evil thoughts. *Ouch!* That's not fun to think about. But again, it's true. I think bad things about a person who doesn't wear clean clothes, like: *She needs to take better care of herself.* Or *I smell something funny . . . it must be her.* And, *Oh, Lord, please don't make me go talk to her. She probably just wants some money.* Again, that's painful to admit, but it's true. And again, it's probably true for you, too.

What if a girl came into your youth group one Wednesday night wearing obvious hand-me-downs, had greasy hair, and dirty nails? What would you think? What conclusions would you draw about her? It's time to be honest.

Write down what would be going through your mind. What do your thoughts reveal about your heart and the kinds of snap judgments you are capable of making? Journal about it all in the space provided below.

✳ RICH IN FAITH

Following James' example about the finely dressed man and the poor man, James set out to explain why showing favoritism was wrong.

Read James 2:5-8 to discover what issues James pointed out and complete the work below:

✳ God chose the poor to be

_____ in

_____

✳ What does that mean, practically? How have you seen that in your life or world?

✳ What three things did the rich do to the Christians to whom James was writing? See verses 6-7.

1. _____ you

2. _____ you into

_____

3. _____ the

_____

that you bear

In these verses, James reminded the church at Jerusalem (and us!) that God chose the poor to be rich in faith and to be heirs in His kingdom. *Wait, you're saying, doesn't that mean that God is showing favoritism to the poor by choosing them?* Of course not. God is impartial. He is just; He is fair.

Think about it this way: In Matthew 5:3, Jesus said, "The poor in spirit are blessed, for the kingdom of heaven is theirs." The poor in spirit are those who know they need a Savior, know they cannot earn their own salvation, know that they must rely on God's grace and mercy for everything. We can all be poor in spirit—and we all are when we recognize our desperate need for a Savior.

But it's also true that the poor in Spirit are also those who are economically poor. Many times, it is the poor who respond to the message of the gospel because they know they need a Savior. They know what it is to really need something—and they know that they can't save themselves. Jesus' statement is a play on words that used both meanings—poor in spirit and poor economically. God isn't playing favorites. Anyone can be a part of the kingdom of God. But many times, the rich don't recognize that they need anything, and therefore they reject the gospel message (Matt. 6:19-24).

That was really happening to James' original audience. As James went on to explain in these verses, these rich people were actually exploiting the Jewish Christians to whom he was writing. The rich were oppressing the poor believers, taking them to court to get their money. They belittled these Christ-followers precisely because they followed Him. Yet, despite this mistreatment, the believers were still showing favor to these rich people.

✳ X-RAY VISION

Perhaps you don't show favoritism to rich people. Maybe you struggle in other areas. If God were to take an x-ray of your heart, where would He find your weaknesses? Where (or to whom) do you show favoritism?

Draw a line from the area of weaknesses you have to the heart in the center.

pretty girls

the popular crowd

cheerleaders

people who fit in

cute guys

people you've known forever

smart people

people a lot like you

strong Christians

the prom queen

atheists

star athletes

gay people

skinny girls

people of a different race or social class

techy people

✳ Take a look at the kinds of people you identified. Are there some people you choose NOT to favor because of a certain trait of theirs? Do you avoid smart girls because you think they're not cool? Do you dislike the people who fit in because you don't, or atheists because they don't believe like you do? Put a box around the kinds of people on the list you discriminate against. Add others to the list as the Holy Spirit reveals them to you.

Tomorrow, you will learn about James' solution for favoritism. For now, spend some time asking God to create in you a heart that values what He values. Ask Him to develop in you a love that mirrors His love. And spend some time thanking Him for not showing partiality against you, but loving you in your sin and offering you eternal life regardless of your past, your gender, your ethnicity, or your faithfulness to Him. Thank Him for being just and merciful.

✳ If you'd prefer, journal your prayer in the space provided below.

TRAINING MANUAL

Today, you'll read James 4. Use the following outline to help guide your interaction with Scripture as the Holy Spirit speaks to you.

WEEK 3

* Pray.

* Read the entire chapter.

* Paraphrase the major points of this chapter. List them below:

* What is God telling you about Himself in these verses? Why is that important?

* What is God telling you about yourself and/or others in James 4? How does that challenge you?

* What steps will you take today to respond to what God has revealed to you about your life and yourself in these verses?

Mercy triumphs.

Laws matter. Without them, any culture would turn chaotic. However, some laws are enacted without any thought of a distant future when they probably would no longer be needed.

Listed below are some crazy laws. Circle the ones you think are real.

In LaCrosse, Wisconsin, you cannot display a naked mannequin in a store window.

It is illegal to bathe in Sandy Creek Lake (in Clarke County, Georgia).

You could face up to 25 years in prison for cutting down a cactus in Arizona.

If you're ever traveling to Chicago, don't pack your kite. They're illegal to fly within the city limits.

If you happen to be traveling through North Dakota in a covered wagon, keep in mind that it's illegal for you to shoot an Indian on horseback.

If you're traveling in Youngstown, Ohio, you can take a cab, but it's illegal to ride on the roof.

The truth is that all of these laws are real, believe it or not.[1] Obviously some laws matter more than others. I'd sure hate for police officers to be tied up chasing kite flyers instead of investigating theft.

In his letter to these early Christians, James talked about a law that these believers were to live by—a law that would ensure that what they read in God's Word would be lived out in their actions.

Read James 2:8-13. Complete the activities below.

✳ According to James, which law should believers carry out? (See v. 8.)

✳ Why do you think James called it a "royal law"?

✳ This law is actually Jesus' own words. Where did Jesus identify this law? (You'll need to do a little digging in your Bible's concordance to find the Scripture.)

✳ What is the rule of thumb that James introduced in verses 10-11? Fill in the blanks below.

If you _____

_____

_____ then

you _____

_____.

James told us to

_____ and

_____

using the law of freedom as our guide (v. 12).

✳ What is this "law of freedom"? What does it mean that we will be judged by it?

✳ What is the rule of thumb James gave us in verse 13?

One who does not _____

_____ will

not _____

_____.

What ultimately triumphs?

_____ Why?

The "royal law" James discussed in verse 8 finds its roots in the Old Testament (Lev. 19:18), but it came alive in Jesus Christ. Nobody knows for sure why it is called "royal" (so there was no right or wrong answer in the activity above), but it could be because Jesus is the King and in His kingdom, we follow His sometimes-upside-down way of life. He put a different spin on the Levitical law when He said our neighbor was anyone who was in need in Luke 10:25-37.

Here's where James made people squirm, though. In effect, he said, "Don't think you're keeping the law of Christ while you are practicing favoritism. It is as much a contradiction if you claimed you were keeping the law just because you were not committing adultery even though you were practicing murder…if you show favoritism, you sin."[2]

Why would he make such a sharp statement? To show that everyone is in need of God's mercy. No one ever keeps all of the commands of the law.

The Jews thought that the law of God was a series of commands that didn't relate to each other. To keep one part of the law earned God's favor, even if you broke another law while doing it. People saw the law as a balance sheet—you added up the good and subtracted the bad, hoping to emerge with more good. Sounds a little like our world today, doesn't it? Most people would say, "I am a pretty good person. It's not like I've murdered anybody." Or "I go to church and I don't use God's name in vain, so I'm OK." But James effectively destroyed that fantasy in today's Scripture passage by reminding us that if we break one law—or one part of one law—it means we're lawbreakers. Period.

We are all guilty of sin. Not one of us can claim that we've never broken any of the laws or standards set out by God. That's part of how we know we need a Savior. And when you recognize your desperate need for a Savior, you also acknowledge the weight of sin that keeps us from truly being free.

Read John 8:31-32.

* Based on these verses, what or who will set us free?

* How do we obtain such freedom? Read John 8:36 to find out.

* How does the Son set you free?

In Romans 8:1-2, Paul explains that Christ Jesus sets us free from "the law of sin and of death." When He died on the cross, paying the penalty of our sin (which would have been eternal damnation), He set us free to live in eternity with Him later and in fellowship with Him now.

Because He has set us free, redeemed us, and recreated us (2 Cor. 5:17), we can offer the same mercy to others that has been given to us. He sets us free from judging others on the basis of money or skin color or popularity or intelligence or weight. Because we have been accepted in Christ on no merit of our own, we can accept others.

✱ BUT WAIT!

If you and I have received mercy from God in the death and resurrection of Jesus, then how could James write what he did in verse 13?

Just for review, summarize that verse here:

So does that mean we can lose our place in heaven if we play favorites sometimes? That God won't show us mercy if we don't give mercy? How can we be saved by grace (Eph. 2:8) and yet be denied God's mercy, as this verse seems to suggest?

Remember, James was giving examples of what it was like to live out God's Word in practical ways. He talked about taking care of orphans and widows and remaining unpolluted by the world's system of doing things (Jas. 1:27); he gave the example of showing favoritism (2:1-7) and of loving your neighbor (v. 8). In that same light, James was giving us another example of what it looks like to live out God's Word in James 2:13. Showing mercy is another aspect of true religion (1:27).

James was saying this: if you don't demonstrate mercy to others, then it's obvious that you have never really plunged into the depths of God's mercy. When you come face-to-face with the depth of your sin and the depth of God's grace despite the enormity of your sin, then you will offer mercy to others.

If your life is marked by harsh, judgmental attitudes and criticism of others at every chance, then you probably have never received God's mercy in the first place. And because you have rejected God's mercy, you remain under judgment (John 3:17-18).

Here's the good news: in Christ, mercy triumphs over judgment. God's love and grace through Christ conquer sin and judgment.

✱ RESPONDING TO GOD'S MERCY

Maybe you've never thought about the depths of God's mercy before and have not accepted His offer of forgiveness through His Son. If not, then take the time to reflect on where you are in your journey. What questions do you have? What keeps you from accepting that mercy? Journal in the space provided. Then talk to someone who knows what it means to live a life of faith.

If you are already a follower of Christ, take this time to reflect on God's mercy that saves you and keeps you, even as you read this. Journal your thoughts about God's mercy. And write a prayer of thanks that you didn't get what you deserved—judgment and condemnation for your sin—but instead received the amazing, powerful, transforming, healing love of God.

1. DumbLaws.com [online], cited 6 July 2011. Available from the Internet: *http://www.dumblaws.com/random-laws*

2. Stulac, George M., *James: The IVP New Testament Commentary Series*. (Downers Grove, Ill.: InterVarsity Press, 1993), 103.

TRAINING MANUAL

Today, you'll read James 5. Use the following outline to help guide your interaction with Scripture as the Holy Spirit speaks to you.

* Pray.

* Read the entire chapter.

* Paraphrase the major points of this chapter. Did you notice anything different from your previous readings of this chapter?

* What is God telling you about Himself in James 5?

* What is God telling you about yourself and/or others in these verses?

* What steps will you take to act on what God has revealed to you in these verses?

week four

ACTIVE

✳ Faith Under Pressure: Active

➡ The person who makes it, sells it. The person who buys it never uses it, and the person who uses it doesn't know they are. What is it?

➡ You throw away the outside and cook the inside. Then, you eat the outside and throw away the inside. What did you eat?

➡ What always runs but never walks, often murmurs, never talks, has a bed but never sleeps, has a mouth but never eats?

Pose any of these questions to a group of friends, and you'll have that group pondering the answers for hours. They'll try to answer the questions (and most won't get them right), try to bribe or blackmail you into telling them, and groan when they can't think of the "simple" answer you'll finally give them. *(In case you're wondering, the answers are: a coffin, an ear of corn, and a river.)*

In the passage of Scripture you'll dig into this week, James 2:14-26, James used questions as a way to make a point. The questions he asks in these verses might seem a bit tricky at first, but fortunately, he had a definite answer in mind as he made his point. And unlike the questions you just read, James' questions—and their answers—have eternal significance.

Faith and works

Read James 2:14 and list the two questions that James asks:

1.

2.

⁎ What point do you think James was trying to make by asking these questions? (You'll have to think!)

Before we dig into these questions, let's make sure we're all on the same page by defining a couple of key words James used in this verse: *faith* and *works*. James used these words throughout the rest of this chapter, so we need to make sure that we know what he means by *faith* and *works* now so we're not confused later.

How do you define the word <u>faith</u>?

How do you define the word <u>works</u>?

Using your definitions from above, paraphrase the verses you just read:

"What good is it, my brothers, if someone says he has _____, but does not have _____? Can his _____ save him?

⁎ Do your definitions help you to better understand these verses, or do they add to your confusion? Why?

Some people reading these verses might mistakenly think that James was saying that a person is saved by works rather than by faith. In fact, some denominations use this verse to show that a person must earn his or her way into heaven by doing good works. If that is the case, then what James said contradicted what Paul said in several places in the New Testament.

Read the following Scriptures and write down what each says about faith and how you are saved from your sin.

✴ Acts 16:31

✴ Romans 3:28

✴ Romans 5:1

✴ Ephesians 2:8-9

✴ Based on these verses, were Paul and James contradicting each other? Explain your answer.

✴ If not, then how do you explain the differences in what each one wrote about faith and works in Scripture?

✴ PAUL VS. JAMES

James and Paul did not contradict each other. They were just looking at different times or points in the same faith journey. Paul was looking at the very beginning of the faith process, the point in time in which a person turns from sin and turns to God for forgiveness.

You and I can never do enough stuff to earn God's grace. That's why we have to accept it by faith. God must do all the work—declaring us righteous because of Jesus' death on the cross. This is called justification.

In the Scripture you read today, James was looking at a different point in the faith journey, the point at which a person's life should be marked by change because of the work God has done and is doing in her life. We become a new creation (2 Cor. 5:17). This process of becoming more like Jesus (Rom. 8:29) is called sanctification. Part of that process is a change in lifestyle—sometimes called works.

Think of it this way: works (or deeds or actions or whatever you want to call them) are done **because** of your faith in Jesus Christ not **instead** of your faith in Jesus Christ. Acting is a result of already being accepted by God's grace, not as a means to earn God's grace. Works immediately follow grace. In other words, when you recognize God's grace and become a Christian, it changes the way you live and good works that point to Christ will appear in your life. James wasn't contradicting Paul; James was simply pointing to the evidence of true faith: good works.

✷ BACK TO THE BEGINNING

Let's go back to James' original questions in verse 14. What point was he trying to make? Reading this verse in several translations might help you to better understand it.

First, write out James 2:14 as it is stated in your Bible. Then, read verse 14 again from the various translations shown in the next column. Underline the portions in each that are different from what your Bible said.

YOUR TRANSLATION:

What good is it, my brothers, if someone says he has faith but does not have works? Can his faith save him? (HCSB)

What good is it, my brothers, if someone claims to have faith but has no deeds? Can such faith save him? (NIV)

What is the use (profit), my brethren, for anyone to profess to have faith if he has no good works to show for it? Can such faith save his soul? (Amplified Bible)

Dear friends, do you think you'll get anywhere in this if you learn all the right words but never do anything? Does merely talking about faith indicate that a person really has it? (The Message)

My friends, what good is it to say you have faith, when you don't do anything to show that you really do have faith? Can that kind of faith save you? (Contemporary English Version)

What good is it, dear brothers and sisters, if you say you have faith but don't show it by your actions? Can that kind of faith save anyone? (New Living Translation)

Now that you've heard how others have translated it, summarize the point James was trying to make:

Someone can say they have faith in Jesus. But just saying you believe in Jesus doesn't matter if you don't show it in your actions. That kind of faith isn't the real deal. True faith—that transforming faith that changes you from the inside out because the Holy Spirit comes to reside in you and change you into Jesus' likeness—results in actions.

True faith and works—you'll never find one without the other.

✳ AN INWARD LOOK

A deep discussion like this means nothing if it doesn't require you to look inward at your own life.

What evidence in your life shows that Christ is residing in your heart? Think about it in these three areas:

✳ Devotion (things that keep you in touch with God and nourished by God)

✳ Choices (doing what is right)

✳ Ministry (using your gifts to serve God and others)

The rest of this week, we'll dig deeper into what James meant by faith and actions. For now, pray and ask God to show you whether or not you have an outward evidence of what He is doing inwardly in your heart.

TRAINING MANUAL

Today, you'll read James 1. Use the following outline to help guide your interaction with Scripture as the Holy Spirit speaks to you.

WEEK

* Pray.

* Read the entire chapter.

* What is God telling you about Himself in James 1?

* Paraphrase the major points of this chapter:

* What is God telling you about yourself and/or others in these verses?

* What steps will you take today to apply what God's Word has revealed to you to your life?

Faith in action

Yesterday, you learned the difference between saying you have faith in Jesus and actually having a living, active faith in Him. Saying you believe in Jesus is not just an intellectual agreement—it's a belief that results in action.

For instance, I can agree that 10 x 10 = 100. That belief doesn't influence or affect my behavior in any way (other than getting an answer correct on a math quiz). On the other hand, if I agree that ten $10 bills make up $100, then I would speak up if a cashier only gave me eight $10 bills in exchange for a $100 bill. That belief directed my actions.

Think about it like this: you're on a hiking trip in the Blue Ridge Mountains. You come upon an old, rickety bridge that connects two hills across a steep valley. There are hundreds of feet between you and the bottom of the valley. You could stand on one side of that old, worn-out bridge and agree that it could support your weight if you stepped onto it. That's intellectual assent. But if you actually set foot on that bridge, you have just acted on what you believe.

That's just one example. Think about your own life. What situation would show the difference between saying you believe a truth and actually acting on that truth? Write or draw it below:

✳ JAMES' ANALOGY

James provided an analogy to help his readers better understand why there must be an active element to their belief in Jesus; it isn't just *saying* you believe in Him.

Read James 2:15-16. Then, connect each of the phrases on the left with its definition or paraphrase on the right:

"brother or sister"	you do nothing
"without clothes and lacks daily food"	basic human needs
	I hope you find clothes and food
"go in peace"	it is useless to say
"keep warm, and eat well"	a fellow Christian
"you don't give"	have a nice day
"what the body needs"	
"what good is it"	has a real need

When James used the phrase "brother or sister" in verse 15, it wasn't just a coincidence that he chose words that implied a relationship. James wanted his original readers (and us) to understand that when he said "brother or sister," he meant someone you know, a fellow Christian, not a nameless face. It's not just a random person you might see on a TV commercial or a picture in a magazine. It's someone you know; someone with whom you have some sort of relationship. James was referring to the people around you, real people who have real needs. And in the case of James' original audience, those people were probably also poor, because of the persecution they were facing. These people needed help.

✳ Think about your own life. Who are real people in your life who have real needs? Think of people at school, on a sports team with you, in your church, or at work. List their names and needs.

Person	Needs

What would those real people think or believe if you said something like, "I am so sorry you don't have any food. I hope you can find some and it works out for you"?

Let's make that example a little more personal. Say you broke your leg playing soccer over the weekend. You hobble into the cafeteria and stand in line. As you're hobbling on your crutches and trying to balance your tray of food, a bunch of people come up to you and say, "Oh, I'm so sorry! Can I sign your cast?" Then, they walk away. Would you think those people really cared? Did they mean it when they said, "I'm so sorry!"? Why or why not?

Nobody who has an ounce of compassion or concern for you would just sign your cast and walk away. If she really cared, she would grab your tray and help you to your table.

✳ JESUS' EXAMPLE

As a believer, your belief should lead to an action. Why? Because you model your Savior.

Read the Scriptures below. Match the thing Jesus said with the action that He took to demonstrate that belief.

What Jesus Said	What Jesus Did
Matthew 5:6-7	John 9:1-7
Matthew 5:43-44	Luke 19:1-10
Luke 4:18-21	Matthew 14:23
Luke 5:31-32	Luke 23:34

✳ ONE LAST STATEMENT

James summed up his analogy by making a bold statement.

✳ Read it in James 2:17 and jot down what you think James meant:

The NIV says, "In the same way, faith by itself, if it is not accompanied by action, is dead." The New Living Translation renders this verse as, "So you see, faith by itself isn't enough. Unless it produces good deeds, it is dead and useless." And *The Message* paraphrases the verse to say, "Isn't it obvious that God-talk without God-acts is outrageous nonsense?"

The point? **Faith without actions is useless.** James wasn't saying that actions matter more than faith, but rather he was warning his readers (and us) that true belief in Jesus means that our lives should be marked by a demonstration of surrendering to His command to help others in need.

Read the following paragraph and respond below it:

"There is nothing more dangerous than the repeated experiencing of a fine emotion with no attempt to put it into action. It is a fact that every time we feel a generous impulse without taking action, we become less likely ever to take action. In a sense, it is true to say that we have no right to feel sympathy unless we at least attempt to put that sympathy into action."[1]

✳ Which statements stick out to you the most?

✳ What is God prompting you to do?

✳ What steps will you take to respond to God's prompting today?

1. Wiliam Barclay, *The Letters of James and Peter*, (Louisville, Ky.: Westminster John Knox Press, 2003), 87.

TRAINING MANUAL

Today, you'll read James 2. Use the following outline to help guide your interaction with Scripture as the Holy Spirit speaks to you.

✳ Pray.

✳ Read the entire chapter.

✳ Paraphrase the major points of this chapter. Compare your findings to what you wrote last week (p. 71).

✳ What is God telling you about Himself? What new things did God bring to your attention in this week's reading of James 2?

✳ What is God telling you about yourself and/or others in this passage?

✳ What steps will you take today to respond to what God has revealed to you in these verses?

Faith without works is dead.

When I was in high school, I wrote for my school's newspaper and represented that paper at writing competitions. One of the key principles drilled into my head during my time on staff was that in every editorial, a writer should present her thoughts or position on a subject and why she believes it, like why she thinks secondhand smoke is dangerous, for example. Then, a good editorial writer must present any objections that a person might have with her opinion and prove that person wrong with fact, example, or logic. So if she was writing an editorial about secondhand smoke, she might say something like: "Some may say that secondhand smoke dissipates in the air, but statistics show…"

James' statements in the passage of Scripture we'll focus on today sound very much like he and I studied under the same journalism teacher.

* In James 2:18-19, James presented a hypothetical opponent who disagreed with him. In the spot provided, write out the gist of what that person would say to James.

In these verses, James' presents an argument from a hypothetical opponent who is arguing against James' teaching that faith and action go hand in hand. That person would say to James, "You have faith, and I have works" (v. 18). In other words, that you could possess one or the other (but not necessarily both, and each was an acceptable approach to God. In this fictional person's opinion, one person can choose to have belief in God and focus on that, while another person may focus on actions (aka "works").

The person who focuses on just belief in God might say, "I believe in God but I don't do all that church stuff." Or, "I think God created this world but isn't involved with it anymore." Perhaps she would say, "I believe God exists." Such a person acknowledges God as real, but nothing more.

On the other hand, a person who focuses on works might say, "Helping people is more important than following some stupid religious rules." Or, "I just try to live a good life. And I pay my taxes. I do my part. I help the environment. That's what matters— making the world better."

✴ JAMES' REBUTTAL

James had something to say about that. Like any good editorial writer, James showed the flaw in this argument by asking his fictional opponent to show one thing.

* What was it?

* What was James' response? How would you say that in your own words? Write it below.

James' argument was simple: show me your faith without any works. Try it. Can you demonstrate faith without an action attached? Nope. It can't be done. You don't have faith in something or someone or even God if you're not willing to take action because of what you believe.

That's James' point. That's why he said, "I will show you my faith from my works." In other words, he was saying, "Prove that you have faith without doing kind deeds, and I will prove that I have faith by doing them" (v. 18, CEV).

✱ JAMES' STARK EXAMPLE

As if he hadn't proven his point well enough already, James gave an even more convincing argument for the connection between faith and works. It's found in verse 19.

Write it here:

✱ What did James mean when he wrote, "God is one"? *(Check out Deut. 6:4-5 for your answer.)*

✱ What comparison did James make to the person who said they believed in God without acting on that belief? Why is that important? How does it challenge you?

Deuteronomy 6:4-5 is a basic creed in Judaism, so James' original audience knew it by heart. They knew that it was a proclamation that Yahweh, the God of the Old Testament and the God James spoke of, was the one true God. Everything else was a false god. The Jews gave allegiance to and put their faith and trust in this God, the one true God.

James had a reason for bringing that up. He admitted that it was good that his readers understood that God was the one true God. However, James also wanted them to understand that anyone who claimed to know God without acting on that knowledge (that He was the one true God) failed to read, hear, and heed the *whole* creed. It was good that they believed in the one true God; but that was also a weak faith, a faith that didn't go very far and required little of them.

✱ WHAT DEMONS BELIEVE

I appreciate sarcasm and to me, James comes across as a little sarcastic in verse 19. I mean, he basically said, "You believe in God. Great. So do the demons." He was obviously using irony to show them the foolishness in their thinking. But where did he get his ideas about what demons believe?

Read the following Scriptures. Next to each, jot down what you learn about demons.

✱ Matthew 8:28-29   ✱ Mark 5:7   ✱ Luke 4:41

You probably learned from your reading in three of the four Gospels, that the demons acknowledged God—they recognized Jesus as the Son of God—but in no instance did a demon repent and turn to Jesus. Even though demons believe in the existence of God, they don't produce good works. That's an important warning to those of us who claim to follow Christ: You can say all the right things and agree to a right truth and still have an evil character.

✳ BIBLICAL EXAMPLE

James wasn't the only person in Scripture to highlight the importance of actions that accompany belief. In fact, his Savior (and ours) talked about belief and action very early in His ministry.

Check out Matthew 7:17-23 and complete the activity below.

✳ According to Jesus, how would you recognize a tree? *(See verse 16.)*

✳ What produces good fruit?

✳ What produces bad fruit?

✳ What is impossible, according to Jesus? *(See verse 18.)*

✳ What did He say about people who say "Lord, Lord"?

✳ What does the word "Lord" mean, anyway?

✳ What was missing from their lives?

Good trees bear good fruit. Bad trees bear bad fruit. You'll recognize a tree by the fruit hanging from its branches, and you'll recognize a person by the fruit of their lives. The very word Lord means "master" or "ruler," implying something significant: if Jesus is the Lord of your life, He is in control. He calls the shots. A person can call Jesus "Lord" and never know Jesus personally. The action may be there (prophesying, calling out demons, doing miracles), but if the heart and will aren't surrendered to God, that's just works without genuine faith.

Think about your own life. Are you doing all the right things, but without having an inward change of your heart? Ask the Holy Spirit to confirm your surrender to God or convict you for never really giving your heart to Him. What is He saying to you?

✱ DIFFERENT SIDE, SAME COIN

John, the disciple of Jesus and the writer of 1, 2, and 3 John, also talked about the marriage of faith and works.

Read the passage below and underline what John said about belief and action:

The one who says, "I have come to know Him," yet doesn't keep His commands, is a liar, and the truth is not in him. But whoever keeps His word, truly in him the love of God is perfected. This is how we know we are in Him: one who says he remains in Him should walk just as He walked. —1 John 2:4-6

The point? Living faith results in action. An experience or memory of giving your life to Jesus Christ is not in itself proof that you have been saved. The only outward proof of an inward transformation through God's Spirit is the life that you live after you have given your heart and life to Jesus. You cannot claim to be a true follower of Jesus if your life hasn't changed and there's no godly fruit hanging in your life.

Close this time of study in God's Word by allowing God's Spirit to show you the evidence in your life that your heart has been changed. Ask Him to confirm your life of faith and works, or to convict you that you show no evidence of a changed life. What is He saying to you?

Journal your thoughts or prayer below:

TRAINING MANUAL

Today, you'll read James 3. Use the following outline to help guide your interaction with Scripture as the Holy Spirit speaks to you.

✷ Pray.

✷ Read the entire chapter.

✷ Paraphrase the major points of this chapter:

✷ What is God telling you about Himself in James 3? How do your findings compare to last week's (p. 76)?

✷ What is God telling you about yourself and/or others in these verses?

✷ What steps will you take to respond to what God has said to you through His Word?

 *Amazing faith*

What would you do to demonstrate your love for someone? **Take this quiz just to test your willingness.**

✳ Would you . . .

_____ Eat a chocolate-covered cricket?

_____ Move to another country?

_____ Give up chocolate?

_____ Shave your head in support of a cancer patient?

_____ Leave your family and never see them again?

_____ Change religions?

_____ Give up your dream career?

_____ Skydive?

_____ Get a tattoo?

_____ Donate a kidney?

_____ Kill your child?

Most of us would make sacrifices to show someone we loved them. But one man was willing to allow his child to be the sacrifice. We'll learn about such a sacrifice today.

✳ FATHER AND ROLE MODEL

James wanted to provide a powerful example of what a person would do to demonstrate his faith and love.

Read James 2:20-24 and complete the activity below by answering the basic questions.

✳ Who was the hero of the story?

✳ Why was he called "father"?

✳ What actions earned him high esteem in James' opinion?

* What nickname did James give him in verse 23?

* What did James mean when he said that Abraham's faith was "perfected"?

* If you were Abraham and God asked the same thing of you, would you be able to do it? Explain.

The hero of today's story is Abraham, who is considered one of the Patriarchs (fathers) of the Israelites, whose story makes up a large portion of the Old Testament. In fact, Abraham (or Abram in his earliest years) started it all. As Christians, we can look at these early followers of God as our ancestors in the faith, people who walked this road before us. In Abraham's case, his willingness to obey God at the cost of his son's life provides an amazing story of faith.

✳ YOU WANT WHAT?

In case you aren't familiar with the story of Abraham and Isaac, take a few minutes to stop and read Genesis 22:1-19. Don't worry about the tiny details. Just get the overall picture.

* Who was involved:

* What God asked:

* Where they went:

* What they took:

* What they talked about:

* Who tied up Isaac:

* How the story ended:

* What the angel said:

When I reflect on this story, I am astounded by Abraham's obedience that was born out of his faith in God. My husband and I adopted our daughter from Guatemala when she was almost 6 months old. For weeks after she came home to us, I would wake up in the middle of the night in a panic because I couldn't hear her through the monitor. To be able to sleep again, I'd get up, walk across the house to her room, and quietly peek in to make sure she was OK. Even now, I tear up at the thought of losing her. To be authentic and truthful, I don't know if I could be as obedient as Abraham if God asked me to sacrifice my daughter.

✻ ONE + ONE = THREE

James said that "faith was active together with his [Abraham's] works, and by works, faith was perfected" (v. 22). *The Message* says that, "Faith and works are yoked partners, that faith expresses itself in works." If he lived in my house, James would say that they went together like peanut butter and chocolate, two items that are good separately, but when you put them together, they are fantastic! The result is better because the two elements were combined.

That's the point James was making here. Faith and action by themselves are incomplete—it is the interaction between the two that results in amazing things. The two build off of each other and grow each other in an endless cycle, a bit like this:

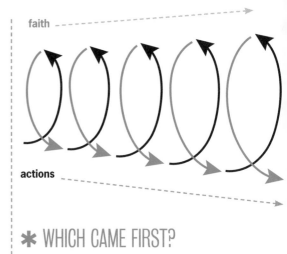

faith

actions

✻ WHICH CAME FIRST?

Reread James 2:23 and summarize what it says in the space provided:

In your Bible, the sentence, "Abraham believed God, and it was credited to him for righteousness" might be in bold letters (it is in mine), or it may be offset in some other way. That means that this particular verse is being quoted from somewhere else in the Bible. In this case, the verse comes from the Old Testament. Let's dig a little deeper into that fact.

Read Genesis 15:1-6 and complete the conversation as if it were a skit. It's been started for you:

✻ Narrator: God came to Abram and said…

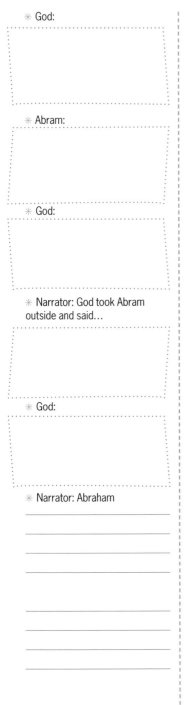

* God:

* Abram:

* God:

* Narrator: God took Abram outside and said...

* God:

* Narrator: Abraham

This story predates the Scripture you read about Abraham and Isaac. In fact, this event in Abram's life takes place at least 30 years before his testing in Genesis 22. So, why is this significant?

Because it shows us that faith came first. And faith was the basis for God calling him righteous. That faith gave evidence 30 years later. That's why James said, "a man is justified by his works and not by faith alone" (2:24). His actions didn't earn him right standing with God. They just demonstrated the faith that was already active in Abraham's life.

For you and me, that means that our actions don't earn us right standing with God. But they do show that a change has taken place in our lives. Our obedience to God demonstrates the authenticity of our faith.

✲ IN PROCESS

There's one little element about Abraham's life that I want you to see. It takes place in Genesis 16, just a chapter after God said Abraham was righteous. **Read Genesis 16:1-5.**

Did you catch what happened in that story? In Genesis 15, God had promised to give Abram/ Abraham as many offspring as the stars in the sky (that's a lot of family!). So what did Abraham do in the next chapter, the one you just read? He panicked. His wife convinced him that God had prevented her from having children and that he should try to have children through their slave, Hagar.

The point? Abraham wasn't perfect. His faith wavered. And yet, James used him as an example of a man of faith whose life showed what he really believed.

God will take you right where you are. He does not demand perfection. He knows that we will falter, stumble, and struggle on our journeys of faith. He will take us no matter where we are, but He also wants to move us forward in our faith. Are you willing to go forward, right where you are? Then get ready for an amazing journey ahead.

TRAINING MANUAL

Today, you'll read James 4. Use the following outline to help guide your interaction with Scripture as the Holy Spirit speaks to you.

* Pray.

* Read the entire chapter.

* What is God telling you about Himself in James 4?

* Paraphrase the major points of this chapter:

* What is God telling you about yourself and/or others in today's reading of these verses? How does that compare to what He's shown you in this chapter previously?

* What steps will you take to respond to what God has taught you today?

Faith involves action.

You've made it through another week! Great work. Engaging in God's Word is a lot like exercise—while you're in the midst of it, it can seem a little painful, but it's all worth it in the end!

Look back over the week's work and summarize it in one sentence below:

My answer would be something like: *faith and works are two sides of the same coin working together to mature you in your relationship with God.* That's the essence of this week's encounter with Scripture. Let's take a look at one more story that will help illustrate this principle and encourage you.

Read James 2:25-26. Who is the main character, and what did she do?

✳ OPENING SCENE

Read Joshua 2:1-7. Think of this story as a movie (it would make a good one!). Summarize the plot to this point. Make sure to list the characters, actions, conflict, and other important elements.

The movie would open with two men, dressed in disguises, looking to infiltrate a city just inside a foreign country's border to gather information about overthrowing it. The authorities get wind of the spies' presence and send men to investigate. Stopping at the house of a prostitute (the last place two God-fearing Israelite men would be!), the authorities tell the woman with questionable morals to send out these men who are allegedly hiding in her home. She lies to the authorities, sending them in another direction, while the men stay safely hidden in her house. The scene ends.

You might not be familiar with the story of Rahab, especially if you're a little rusty on your Old Testament history (like me). Fortunately, the person who wrote the Book of Joshua gives us the backstory.

Who was this woman? We don't know much about her yet, except that she was a prostitute and wasn't afraid to lie to men in high places. But something is different and intriguing about her. Why would she have hidden the spies?

✳ RAHAB'S DECLARATION

✳ Joshua 2:8-16 tells us more about her. Read it carefully and write down everything she says about God in the verses.

✳ What request did Rahab make of the two spies?

Keep in mind where this story takes place. It's in the land of Canaan, which until then, had been a pagan world. The people there didn't follow Yahweh—the one true God—but instead, they worshiped any number of gods, the most popular of which was Baal. And yet, Rahab made some strong, declarative statements about the God of the Israelites. She acknowledged Yahweh as the one true God and decided to trust her future with Him and his people.

Rahab didn't have a Jewish background. She had grown up in a culture of pagans and immorality. She hadn't been to Sunday School all of her life. Because she believed in God, she put her life on the line for the people of God. If her deception had been discovered, she would have been executed for treason. She demonstrated her faith by acting on it. She could have said, "I hope you guys don't get caught. Good luck." But that's not faith.

Faith involves risk.

✳ HOW DOES IT END?

Rahab risked everything and trusted her family and her future to the God of the Hebrews. So how does the movie end? What happened to Rahab?

Read Joshua 6:22-25 and record how the conflict was resolved:

God showed up. He was faithful. Through the actions of Joshua and the original two spies, Rahab and her family were spared when the entire city of Jericho was burned. Rahab risked everything because of her faith in God, and God used her for His purposes.

I just love a happy ending.

✱ WHAT HAPPENED TO HER?

There are some clues in Scripture about what happened to Rahab after that, though. One shows up in Joshua 6:25. The writer recorded that Rahab "lives in Israel to this day". Apparently, she maintained her faith in Yahweh. That's all we need to know.

But she is mentioned in two other verses in the entire Bible—two pretty important verses.

Read them and write down what you find out about Rahab.

✳ Matthew 1:5

✳ Hebrews 11:31

Yes, she was mentioned in the lineage of Jesus. Turns out she married a guy named Salmon, had children, and out of that genealogy came King David. What an amazing story of God redeeming a life! Think about it: Rahab was a prostitute, a

profession you wouldn't expect to see in the lineage of God's only Son.

Her story is so remarkable that she was also mentioned in Hebrews 11, which records the lives of the heroes of faith. She is mentioned in the same breath as Abraham and Isaac, Moses and Gideon, Sarah and David. Rahab the prostitute became a model of faith. Think about how God worked in her life.

✳ How does Rahab's story encourage and challenge you? Jot down some thoughts below.

✱ A BODY WITHOUT BREATH

James used one final analogy to complete his thoughts about the importance of faith and deeds working together.

Read James 2:26 and complete the formula below:

A body - _____ = Faith - _____

This verse reminds me of Genesis 2:7, which reads:

Then the Lord God formed the man out of the dust from the ground and breathed the breath of life into his nostrils and the man became a living being.

Life and spirit created a living being. Without the breath of God, Adam was just a big dirt sculpture. In the same way, faith without works is dead. Lifeless. Meaningless. Useless. The things you do because you believe God and His Word breathe life into your faith. Dwell on that for a minute. Let it sink in.

✷ SO WHAT?

This week has been an extensive search into the importance of faith and action, the interplay between the two, and the futility of one without the other. So what? What difference will it make on Monday morning in math class?

Maybe it would be helpful to think a little more practically. There are lots of things you believe in God's Word, but have you connected those beliefs to your actions?

Listed below are several truths in God's Word. Read each one (and the provided Scripture reference if you need more information) and think about how each should affect the way you live your life. Write your ideas and thoughts next to each truth.

✷ Because God created me (Ps. 139), I ...

✷ Because God created others, I ...

✷ Because I cannot serve both God and money (Matt. 6:24), I ...

✷ Because Jesus said to love my enemies (Matt. 5:43-45), I ...

＊ Because my body is God's temple (1 Cor. 6:19), I …

＊ Because Satan is trying to devour me (1 Pet. 5:8), I …

＊ Because God's Word is perfect, trustworthy, true, and reliable (Ps. 19:7-9), I …

＊ Because nothing I do for God is useless (1 Cor. 15:58), I …

＊ Based on everything I have learned from Scripture this week, I …

Remember, faith means risk. But the reward is sweet!

TRAINING MANUAL

WEEK
4

Today, you'll read James 5. Use the following outline to help guide your interaction with Scripture as the Holy Spirit speaks to you.

* Pray.

* Read the entire chapter.

* Paraphrase the major points of this chapter:

* What is God telling you about Himself in James 5?

* What is God telling you about yourself and/or others in these verses?

* What has God revealed to you in these verses? What steps will you take to repond to what He has said?

MINDFUL

Faith Under Pressure: Mindful

A bolt of lightning can travel at speeds of 140,000 miles per hour and can reach temperatures near 54,000 degrees Farenheit. One strike has enough energy to light 150,000,000 light bulbs. One storm can generate enough energy in lightning to supply the entire U.S. with electricity for 20 minutes. Lightning strikes can blow your clothes and shoes off as the moisture on your skin rapidly boils and turns to steam (now that's encouraging, isn't it?). No wonder some people become astraphobic—which is just a fancy way of saying they're afraid of lightning. Lightning is a very powerful force.

This week, you'll discover another powerful force. Just like lightning, one strike of this power force can create havoc on countless lives in just seconds. Like lightning, it often strikes without warning. And just like lightning, you need to be aware of its dangers.

What makes this power different than lightning? Its source: you!

What's your life teaching?

Two high school teachers have left an indelible mark on my life.

Paula McNeil taught home economics. Sewing. Cooking. Family dynamics. We even had to carry around a hard-boiled egg for several days as a reminder of what it would be like to have a child (mine broke). She also taught me that it was OK to wear make-up and to dress femininely, two concepts that I never learned from my parents. And she was a Christian. Her brother was killed in an accident just before my senior year, and I learned from her how Christians can grieve with hope.

Anne Gillespie taught journalism. For three years, I soaked up her knowledge of headlines and picas and layouts and inverted pyramid writing. Mostly, though, I gained a passion for words and their power not only to inform, but also to enlighten, encourage, and incite. She was also a Christian and wasn't ashamed for others to know. She was bold, and I admired her for that.

Henry Brooks Adams once said, "A teacher affects eternity; he can never tell where his influence stops." I agree with him. What about you? Who have been some of the most influential teachers in your life?

Jot down their names and why they have meant so much to you:

✳ TEACHERS NOT WANTED?

Believe it or not, James talked about teachers—not teachers in a high school science class, but rather, those who lead you and me in understanding more about God's Word.

Read James 3:1-2 and write down everything James said about teachers:

The Message says:

"Don't be in any rush to become a teacher, my friends. Teaching is highly responsible work. Teachers are held to the strictest standards. And none of us is perfectly qualified. We get it wrong nearly every time we open our mouths. If you could find someone whose speech was perfectly true, you'd have a perfect person, in perfect control of life." —James 3:1-2

* Why is teaching such a "highly responsible work?"

* Why are teachers "held to the strictest standards"?

* Do you think James was discouraging people to become teachers? Why or why not?

Let's go back to last week's truth for a minute. Remember what we learned? **Faith without action is dead.** In other words, your actions demonstrate to others that you have a growing faith relationship with God. So right after James drops that truth on his readers, he starts talking about being teachers in the very next sentence. Huh? What's the connection?

✳ WHO ARE YOU LOOKING AT?

Let me ask a question: Whom do you look up to?

In the space below, list those people and why you look up to them:

How many of those people have taught you something significant? Circle their names. How many of them have been a role model for you, showing you an example of something, from how to pray to how to kick a soccer ball correctly? Circle their names, too.

Those people are meaningful to you because you have learned from them. They have taught you both by word and by action. What they believed was backed up by what they did.

To James, what you believe and what you do leads to what you teach. And to him, not many people should be teachers. Why? Because it's a heavy, heavy responsibility. Perhaps Jesus' words in Matthew 5:18-20 were still ringing in his ears.

Read Matthew 5:18-20 and summarize those verses here:

Jesus understood that words are meaningless if actions don't back them up. That's why Jesus talked about the scribes and Pharisees with such negative tones in the passage of Scripture you just read. They taught the law, but they didn't live what they taught—which is basically the definition of the word *hypocrite*. In fact, Jesus called even the scribes and Pharisees hypocrites. In Matthew 23:13, Jesus said, "But woe to you, scribes and Pharisees, hypocrites! You lock up the kingdom of heaven from people. For you don't go in, and you don't allow those entering to go in."

What was his point? These so-called teachers were missing out on the kingdom of God because they refused to believe in Jesus. That's what "you don't go in" meant. And, they were causing the people under their care, their students, to miss the Messiah's coming, too. That's what Jesus meant when he said, "you lock up the kingdom of heaven from people." Not only were the scribes and Pharisees missing out on a relationship with Jesus, but they were also making it difficult for others to have that relationship. I would hate for that to be said about me.

✱ WHO'S LOOKING AT YOU?

You might be thinking to yourself, "Whew, I'm glad I'm not a teacher." But, you **are** a teacher, even if you don't lead Bible study on Sunday mornings.

✴ Read 1 Timothy 4:12. Summarize Paul's command:

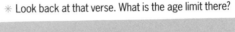

✴ Look back at that verse. What is the age limit there?

You're right. There isn't one. It just says "Let no one despise your youth." Who determines how old youth is? When I was a little girl, I never thought I would turn 30. That was so far away. I genuinely thought that Jesus would return before then. It just seemed such a long time off in the future. Now, being 30 was just a speed bump I zoomed past on my way to 40.

You may feel young. And you are. But others are younger than you, and they look up to you. I know because I am seeing it in action in my daughter's life. I teach a group of teen girls at my church. Every time my daughter sees one of those girls, she lets go of my hand, tears off in a dead run, and leaps into that girl's arms. She is watching those girls—how they interact, how they dress, what they say to me and to other people. They are teaching her without ever standing behind a pulpit.

✴ What about you? Who are those younger than you who look up to you?

* What are they learning from your life?

* Based on today's study, what is God saying to you about your faith and what you're teaching others by how you're living? Did He bring to mind some changes you need to make? List them here and journal your thoughts or prayer below.

Tomorrow, we'll tackle the heart of James 3 and in doing so, tread on some uncomfortable ground. For now, ask God to soften your heart and prepare you for what He wants to say to you in the days to come.

TRAINING MANUAL

Today, you'll read James 1. Use the following outline to help guide your interaction with Scripture as the Holy Spirit speaks to you.

* Pray.

* Read the entire chapter.

* Paraphrase the major points of James 1. What's sticking out to you in light of what you studied today?

* What is God telling you about Himself in these verses? Notice any difference from last week's reading? (See p. 94.)

* What is God telling you about yourself and/or others? How do those things challenge or encourage you?

* What has God revealed to you in these verses? What steps will you take to respond to Him?

 *Watch your mouth!*

WEEK

5

"Sticks and stones may break my bones, but words will never hurt me."

Really? The person who coined that phrase must not ever have been the subject of gossip or snide remarks. That person could **not** have been a girl!

No one knows more about the power of words than a teenage girl. Why? Because teen girls are brutal in the way they gossip, trash talk, and tear each other down.

If you were to rewrite the saying above to correctly reflect what it feels like to be the object of someone's unkind words, how would you write it? Complete the sentence:

Sticks and stones may break

my bones, but words

_____ .

When I was a teenager like you, I wrote a poem. It ended like this:

Sticks and stones may break bones,
But only words can wound the soul.

I believed that then, and I believe it now. Words are powerful. James understood that.

✳ SMALL IN SIZE, BUT BIG IN IMPACT

James talked about the power of words when he talked about teachers, reminding us that we all struggle with our speech. Our mouths get us into trouble! As we walk through the verses for today, please remember that this Scripture is not intended to discourage you, but to challenge you. Yes, honoring God with your speech is difficult, but it is possible.

Read James 3:3-4. Doodle in the space below the point that James was trying to make in these verses.

Small things can have a major impact. A piece of hair in your mouth. A mosquito in your bedroom. A penny in a toddler's mouth. Sand in your bathing suit. Small items can distract, irritate, or even cause havoc. James used a similar idea when he talked about the power of the tongue.

✴ DIRECTION OF YOUR LIFE

Notice the first two illustrations James used—the bit in a horse's mouth and the rudder of a ship. Both are very small items in proportion to the thing they control. Even though each is small, both direct the course of something large.

✴ How can a person's tongue direct her life?

✴ Think about a time when something you said brought hope, healing, or joy to another person. Write down what you said (if you can remember it) and how the other person received it.

✴ Now think about a time when something you said brought pain or discouragement. What happened, and what was the outcome?

✴ NOT-SO-FLATTERING-WORDS

The tongue can direct your life—for good or for bad. The same applies to a fire. In the fireplace, a fire gives warmth. Outside that fireplace, a fire destroys a home. Unfortunately, some of the time, our words are like an out-of-control fire. What we say **can** destroy others.

Read James 3:5-6. Using the prompts below, complete the chart to summarize how James described the path an uncontrolled tongue follows.

Placed among _____, it

_____ the whole body and sets

the course of _____ —set on

fire by_____.

✴ What do you think James was referring to when he used the term "body" in verses 5-6?

✴ Why do you think James used such strong language to describe the power of our words?

Most of the time, when I hear or read the word "body" in Scripture, I think of the body of Christ, or the church. Paul used that term a lot in his letters to different churches. (Check out Rom. 12:4-5 and 1 Cor. 12:4-26 to see what I mean.) James' words in today's Scripture passage make sense if he meant the body of Christ. How many times has a church been destroyed by gossip? How many times has a church been damaged by hateful speech among its members? Clearly, James could be warning you and me (and other members of the church) that the tongue, when let loose on a church, could cause treacherous damage and disunity. It's a warning we should all pay attention to.

But what if James wasn't referring to the church? What if he was talking about an individual's tongue? Then how could we apply verses 5-6?

✳ WHERE ARE YOU HEADED?

In verse 6, James said that the tongue "pollutes the whole body." How could your speech pollute your own body?

Complete the following exercise to sharpen your focus on what James was saying. For each of the scenarios, write down how an action of the tongue could corrupt you as a person:

Action	Possible Corruption
Lying	
Trash talking	
Hateful speech	
Sexually charged speech	
Gossip	
Sarcastic speech	

If you continually lie, you become a person who doesn't value truth and honesty. If you gossip all the time, you get a reputation as a gossip. If you use sexually charged speech around guys, then they won't respect you. See the connection? **An action quickly becomes a habit.**

So what? What difference does it make that you have a bad habit? I chew my nails. It's a bad habit. No big deal, right?

It is a big deal when it comes to sinful choices. James made it clear that what you say with your speech will direct your entire life. Verse 6 reads, "The tongue . . . sets the whole course of his life on fire." How can lying, gossip, or trash talking set the whole direction of your life?

WEEK
5

Look at it this way:

An action becomes a habit.

A habit develops into your lifestyle.

Your lifestyle defines your character.

Your character determines your future.

* Think about the actions from the previous page. How could those actions now determine your character and your future?

Action	Future Character
Lying	
Trash talking	
Hateful speech	
Sexually charged speech	
Gossip	
Sarcastic speech	

✴ IS IT IMPOSSIBLE?

James gave a stern word in verses 7-8. What impossible task did he talk about?

> * Really, it's impossible to tame the tongue? So what's the use?

James wasn't saying that God-honoring speech is impossible. He was saying that left alone, your speech would be "a restless evil." Without actively asking God to help you, what you say would become "full of deadly poison." The key to controlling your speech is in recognizing that you cannot control it by yourself.

> * Read Psalm 141:3 and record the prayer of David in that verse:

Close your time with God this morning by making that prayer your own. Continue to pray it before you leave your room every day.

TRAINING MANUAL

Today, you'll read James 2. Use the following outline to help guide your interaction with Scripture as the Holy Spirit speaks to you.

* Pray.

* Read the entire chapter.

* What is God telling you about Himself in James 2?

* Paraphrase the major points of this chapter:

* What is God telling you about yourself and/or others in these verses? Do you notice anything different from previous readings in light of your study today?

* How will you respond to what God has said to you in these verses? Be specific.

✳ *Consider the source.*

It's Sunday afternoon, and you're eating lunch at your favorite restaurant. You order your food at the counter, and the cashier hands you your cup. You walk over to the drink machine and wait in line behind your big brother who is hogging the machine. You watch as he gets ice and then a soft drink. Then, you step up to do the same. You get your ice—no problem. But when you push the lever to get your soft drink, lemonade comes out. You hate lemonade.

You empty out your cup and try again. Ice. Check. Soft drink? Nope. Lemonade. How can that be possible? You just watched your brother get a soft drink out of that same tap.

Sound crazy? Probably. But that's the same example that James used when he talked about a believer's speech.

✳ Read James 3:9-12 and write the comparisons he used in these verses.

Praising and

Sweet water and

Fig tree can't

Grapevine doesn't

Saltwater spring doesn't

✳ UTTERLY IMPOSSIBLE

The first comparison James made can be found in verse 9. Read that verse and circle the comparison in the activity you just completed.

James' original audience would have recognized and understood the religious term "praise," or *bless*, as some translations render it. Originally, the word *bless* meant *to praise or endow something or someone with honor and good words*. Praising and honoring God was a major portion of Old Testament worship in the temple and in the home.

Read the following Scriptures and jot down what they tell you about the word "bless" or "praise."

✳ Psalm 103:1-5

✳ 1 Chronicles 29:10-13

✳ Psalm 117

✳ Psalm 145:3-5

Obviously, it is right and fitting to bless or praise God. He created us. He rules the world, the nations, and everyone on the earth. He is high above all and His greatness is far beyond us.

But out of that same mouth that praises God also comes cursing. The word *cursing* carries the idea of verbal abuse, especially when you lose your temper. It also means to wish bad things on your enemies or to insult or show disrespect.

What did James find so outrageous? Write it down:

Apparently, James heard the people praising God but also condemning someone who was made in God's image. To him, cursing others was equal with cursing God. Ouch!

And to James, such double-speech was utterly impossible. The phrase "should not be" is used only here in the entire New Testament. The phrase was a strong negative term, meaning that there was no place for this duplicity. It was complete nonsense in James' mind for a person who had been redeemed to allow such unholy speech to come out of her mouth. For James, purity of speech with God and with others was a demonstration of genuine faith.

The people in James' day were guilty of hypocrisy in the way they simultaneously praised God and cursed others. They gave God honor, but treated others with complete dishonor.

What about you? Are you ever guilty of praising one minute and verbally bashing in another? Consider the following scenarios. Mark the ones that you have been guilty of doing.

_____ Worshiping God at church, but yelling at your parents on the way home.

_____ Praying during Sunday School, but talking trash about another girl at the mall that afternoon.

_____ Having a quiet time in the morning, but gossiping about a girl at the lunch table.

_____ Praying before a test, but lying to your teacher about how much you studied.

_____ Singing worship songs, but constantly putting down your brother or sister.

_____ Praying for God to help you be pure, but sending a suggestive text to your boyfriend.

Get the point? If we were honest, we'd all admit that we struggle with this issue. That's why James said, "**We** praise our Lord...and **we** curse men..." (v. 9, emphasis added). The problem is that most of us have gotten comfortable with the hypocrisy. We don't see it as a big deal.

For James, this kind of double-talk was utterly contrary to godly character. There was no place for it. It was intolerable. And for us, sadly, it's the norm.

✱ OTHER COMPARISONS

In today's Scripture passage, James used four other analogies to talk about pure speech. Look back on page 127 and circle the comparison that you like the best.

The people of James' day would have readily related to the comparisons of fresh water to salt water. The areas around the Dead Sea contained salty springs (which makes sense because the Dead Sea contains about 10 times more salt than a normal sea). But north of the Dead Sea, the land contained freshwater springs. Those people knew that you couldn't get fresh water from a saltwater spring. It just doesn't happen.

The land where the people James was writing to lived also produced olives, figs, and grapes, among other crops. The people were familiar with farming and harvest. So, these people completely understood that you couldn't get a fig tree to produce olives. Nor could you get figs from a grape vine. People who farm understand this truth: what you sow, you reap. Period.

✳ I'VE HEARD THAT SOMEWHERE BEFORE

James wasn't presenting a new concept to his congregation. He was merely teaching the people what he had been taught. Let's look into that.

Read Matthew 12:33-37.

✳ Who was speaking?

✳ To whom was He speaking? What did He call them?

✳ What were these people guilty of?

✳ According to Jesus, a tree is known by ＿＿＿＿＿＿.
What does that mean?

✳ The mouth ＿＿＿＿＿＿＿ from the overflow of the ＿＿＿＿＿＿＿. How would you say that in your own words? Write it below:

✳ According to Jesus, for what will you be held accountable?

✳ Jesus said that by your words you would be ＿＿＿＿＿＿＿ or ＿＿＿＿＿＿＿.

Words are powerful.
Jesus wasn't saying that what you say will determine whether or not you will be saved. He was saying that your words demonstrate what's on your heart. And if your life is habitually and completely marked by negative speech, lying, trash-talking, and sexually charged dialogue, then something is wrong.

✳ Based on these verses, what is God saying to you specifically about your speech?

✲ WHAT TO AIM FOR

So what should our speech look like? Sound like? The New Testament gives us the answers.

Read each of the verses and list the characteristics of godly speech:

✳ Colossians 3:16

✳ Ephesians 4:29

✳ Ephesians 4:31-32

✳ 1 Peter 3:15-16

✳ 1 Peter 3:8-9

✳ Which one speaks to the changes you need to make in your own life through God's strength? Write it below as a prayer for this day.

TRAINING MANUAL

Today, you'll read James 3. Use the following outline to help guide your interaction with Scripture as the Holy Spirit speaks to you.

* Pray.

* Read the entire chapter.

* What is God telling you about Himself in James 3?

* Paraphrase the major points of this chapter. What sticks out to you in light of what you studied today?

* What is God telling you about yourself and/or others in this chapter? How does that compare to what you wrote last week? (See p. 103.)

* How has God spoken to your heart in these verses? How will you respond to what He has said?

Wise words

A friend of mine was talking the other day about her mother's ability (or lack thereof) to communicate via text messages. She said that in the beginning, her mom didn't know how to use the space key or any of the punctuation keys, so text messages from her wouldbeinonejumbledupmessalotlikethismyfriendhadtolearnwheretoputpunctuationandperiodstofigureoutwherechangesincoversationtookplace.

Whew! That was hard to type.

When I am reading the Book of James, sometimes I think I'm getting a text message from my friend's mom. I forget that the writer originally intended it to be read as a letter. There were no chapter headings, verse indicators, or paragraph indents like we see today. Some of the things he said to his readers (and to us) seem a little disjointed until you remember that he wasn't concerned with outlining a book—he was pouring out his heart to people he loved in a free-flowing first-century blog.

Today's portion of Scripture is going to feel like James was jumping from one topic to the next. However, when you stop and remember the context of the verses and chapters before and after this section, James' thoughts probably won't seem so disjointed.

✳ A TURNING POINT

In the previous verses, James spent a long time talking about the power of the tongue to do good and to do evil. Before that, he had discussed the importance of faith and works at length. Keep that in mind as you complete the following activity.

Read James 3:13-16.

✳ How would you define wisdom?

✳ According to James, how was a wise person supposed to prove she was wise?

✳ How did James describe wisdom?

✳ What do you think James was trying to say in verse 14?

✳ How do these verses connect with the verses before this (Jas. 2:7-12) and the verses after this (Jas. 4:1-6)?

This portion of chapter 3 marks a shift in the letter. Earlier in the book, James had been focusing on the actions that would demonstrate a person's faith in God—not showing favoritism, controlling the tongue, undefiled religion, persevering in trials. In today's focal passage, James 3:13-18, James started talking about wisdom and these verses really serve as a transition into the topics he'll tackle in chapter 4. For James, the means by which a person was able to do any of those things that demonstrated faith in God was by wisdom from above—God's wisdom. That's why James talked so much about a relationship with God in chapter 4 (things like friendship with God and drawing near to God—you'll see when we get there). In today's verses, it's like James was saying, "In order for you to demonstrate a living, active faith, you will need the wisdom of God. And the wisdom of God comes when you…" and so he continues with the rest of his letter.

✳ BREAKING IT DOWN

These verses contain a lot of different phrases that might be overlooked, misunderstood, or just plain ignored because you and I hear them all the time in church or Bible study.

So, let's break them down a little bit.

✳ Below are some of the key phrases along with some definitions. Match the words with their correct meanings. Hopefully, you'll understand a little more about what James was trying to tell you and me.

Good conduct	That which the Devil would delight in
Wisdom	of the present, material world, with no room for God
Gentleness	mental and emotional ideas of modern man
Selfish ambition	applying truth to everyday life
Earthly	humility; strength under control
Sensual	moral behavior based on God's wisdom
Demonic	looking out for yourself by any means necessary

Here's a breakdown of what those words mean:

✳ **Good conduct** means moral behavior based on God's wisdom.

✳ **Wisdom** is the ability to apply truth to everyday life.

✳ **Gentleness** means humility or meekness. When you're gentle or humble, you submit under the authority and sovereignty of God.

✳ **Selfish ambition** means doing whatever you can for yourself however you want, even if it hurts someone else.

✳ **Earthly wisdom** focuses on this material world and things of this world.

✳ **Sensual wisdom** is wisdom that comes from what humans can think and feel.

✳ **Demonic wisdom** is from the Devil. It results in that which the Devil delights in and is opposite of what God delights in.

James was comparing a life under God's leadership and a life lived by the wisdom the world offers.

Read James 3:13-16 again. In the space provided here, jot down any words, adjectives, or phrases that describe or characterize worldy wisdom and godly wisdom. (You can look at the previous activity for help if you need it.)

* Godly Wisdom

* Worldly Wisdom

* Now that you have the characteristics where they belong, go back and read the list from both categories. Circle the characteristics from both columns that describe you. What did you learn?

✳ DON'T LIE!

James made a stark comment in verse 14.

Look back at page 132 for your thoughts on this verse. Write those thoughts and any additional ones in the space provided.

Basically James was calling us out. If you claim to belong to God but your life is marked by envy and ambition, you are living a lie. Don't say you are living by God's standards and God's wisdom, because you aren't. Ouch! James obviously didn't worry about hurting anyone's feelings.

✳ WHAT'S THE END RESULT?

Look back at the traits of worldly wisdom. Do you want that to define your life? Of course not. No one wants to be known for being self-centered, worldly, and focused on the things of the Devil. That's not on my list of the top things I want to be known for. And it's not the way I want to live my life.

* Check out verse 16 to find out why.

* What does this verse tell you is the end result of living by worldly wisdom?

Yep. Disorder and every kind of evil. The Message translates this as, "Whenever you're trying to look better than others or get the better of others, things fall apart and everyone ends up at the others' throats."
Is that how you want to live your life—in a chaos and constant conflict with others? I hope not!

✱ PUTTING IT ALL TOGETHER

James said a lot in just a few verses. If you were to jot down all that you've learned today in James 3:13-16 in a short paragraph, what would you say?

Write it here:

In order to live out what we say we believe, we must constantly depend on God. True wisdom to live out Truth comes from Him and not from ourselves. Trusting in worldly wisdom and living only for yourself only ends in selfish ambition and a life that would delight the Devil. Living life God's way requires one essential character trait: humility.

Are you willing to admit to God that He is sovereign, that He is in control, and that He knows what's best for your life? Are you willing to submit to His authority, lean on His leadership, and seek to live by His principles? Are you willing to act on what you believe about Him? If not, then you might want to evaluate your relationship with Him.

DAY 4

TRAINING MANUAL

Today, you'll read James 4. Use the following outline to help guide your interaction with Scripture as the Holy Spirit speaks to you.

WEEK
5

* Pray.

* Read the entire chapter.

* Paraphrase the major points of James 4. What new things stuck out to you today? Compare to what you've noted in the previous weeks (pp. 28, 56, 82, 108).

* What is God telling you about Himself in this passage?

* What is God telling you about yourself and/or others in these verses?

* What steps will you take to respond to what God has revealed to you in these verses?

True wisdom brings peace.

I love the movie *Mary Poppins.* There, I've said it. Any nanny who could clean up a playroom with a mere snap of her fingers is my hero. (Just ask my closet which is currently stuffed with stuff.) In the very beginning of the movie, Jane and Michael Banks create their own advertisement (it sounds much better with a British accent) that describes what they want in a nanny: cheery disposition; rosy cheeks; no warts (ewww!); plays games; sweet; pretty; gives treats; not cross or cruel; and witty. Sounds like a great nanny, right?

In our last day studying James 3, James provided a character list of his own—not for nannies, but for true wisdom.

Remember, this part of James is a turning point in the letter. He's challenged people in their faith—not showing favoritism, controlling the tongue, practicing undefiled religion, and persevering in trials. We learned yesterday that the only way that happens is a growing relationship with God in which you and I live by His wisdom—wisdom "from above" (v. 17). (By the way, "from above" is the exact phrase James used in 1:17 to talk about good gifts. Wisdom is one of those good gifts that God gives us.)

Read James 3:17-18. In the spot provided here, list the characteristics of wisdom that James highlighted. Next to each, write the word's definition.

* Remember what wisdom is? Look back on page 41 and write the answer below.

* TRUE VS. FALSE

According to James, applying truth to everyday life comes from God alone (from above). If it's not from God, it's not really wisdom. It's the world's brand of wisdom, and it will not get you far. Think about a time when you made a poor decision. Maybe you went to a party and got yourself into a bad situation. Perhaps you lied to your parents. Or, perhaps you found some questionable pictures of guys online and decided to keep looking at them. In each of those cases, I can guarantee that the wisdom you used to make that decision wasn't wisdom at all. Why? Because it wasn't from God. How do I know? Because those decisions violate the characteristics James listed in verses 17-18. Let's look at those characteristics a little more closely.

✳ WHAT TRUE WISDOM LOOKS LIKE

Reread James 3:17. What's the very first characteristic of wisdom James highlighted? Why do you think he listed it first?

PEACE-LOVING. This sounds a lot like what Jesus said in Matthew 5:9 when he blessed the "peacemakers." The word describes a person who seeks peace between two people who are arguing or struggling against each other. In other words, living in God's wisdom and according to His standards means that our actions bring people together, rather than tearing them apart.

✳ What would peace-loving wisdom look in your life? What situation in your life (or the lives of people you know) needs God's peace-loving wisdom?

PURE. This word actually means that something is free from defilement or impurities. Another word we might use in its place is "holy." So what impurities would make wisdom no longer pure? Self-interest. If you really want to live by God's wisdom, then your interests need to pack their bags and take a long vacation. Living by God's wisdom means you seek His will for your life, not your own.

Why would James list purity first? Because if you're not willing to seek His will instead of your own selfish desires, then you won't find wisdom. And the rest of the characteristics listed won't matter because the wisdom isn't there.

✳ Are you willing to seek wisdom from above and not your own? Explain.

GENTLE. Most of the time, we confuse gentleness with meekness. That's not what James meant here. Some translations say "submissive," but that really doesn't fit what James is trying to say, either. The best description is "sweet reasonableness." True godly wisdom knows how to make allowances with people and how to temper justice with mercy. It echoes James 2:13, which says "mercy triumphs over judgment." This means that sometimes, there are larger issues at stake than rules and regulations. A person who is gentle recognizes that fact and gives others kind consideration, treating them the way she would want to be treated.

✳ Who in your life needs a little gentleness? Who needs a little grace? How have you treated that person?

COMPLIANT. Your Bible may say "submissive." Both of these words sort of get at what James was saying here, but not fully. The word *compliant* means that you're willing to listen and learn. It also means that you're open to reason and that you know when to give up your idea and adopt someone else's. To be compliant means that you know that you don't know everything. You're teachable.

* Would the people in your life say you're teachable? That you are willing to listen and learn? Teachers? Parents? Coaches? Where might be some areas where you need a compliant attitude?

* Who needs your mercy? What action can you take to alleviate someone's suffering, even if she doesn't "deserve" it? (After all, did we ever deserve God's mercy? Think about it.)

WITHOUT FAVORITISM AND HYPOCRISY. The word *favoritism* actually means to not waver or sway, to not be indecisive or inconsistent. It can also mean to be impartial. Sound familiar? Yep, back to treating people honestly and fairly, not based on that person's economic status (Jas. 2:1-7). You will treat people based on God's view of humanity (we're all on equal footing) instead of being inconsistent. One person doesn't get special treatment because of some arbitrary marker such as looks, money, or popularity.

To do so would be hypocritical, the last item on James' list of wisdom's characteristics. The word *hypocritical* comes from two Greek words, "without" and "pretend." The word used to refer to someone who was bad at acting. Get the point? When we live in God's wisdom, we don't pretend we know it all. We don't act one way in one situation and the opposite in another. We don't deceive others in order to get what we want. Instead, God's followers are genuine, honest, and sincere.

FULL OF MERCY AND GOOD FRUITS. In the original language, these two words are connected. They go together like peanut butter and jelly. Or peanut butter and chocolate. Or chocolate and just about anything. (Except broccoli; take my word for it.) First, let's define the words and then decide why they're attached at the hip, so to speak.

To be "full of mercy" means that you have pity for a person who is in trouble, even if the trouble is her own fault. It reflects God's mercy for us. Mercy goes out of the way to ease suffering, even when that suffering is caused by a person's stupid choices. Again, it's a reflection of James 2:13—mercy triumphs over judgment. Why? Because God's mercy found a way to triumph over our judgment.

And that mercy results in action, or "good fruit" as James called it. That's why these phrases are connected. Mercy leads to alleviating the suffering. It's not just an emotion; it takes action.

* Look at your own life. Are you guilty of being hypocritical? Do you pretend? Would others say you are genuine, honest, and transparent? Explain.

✳ THE END RESULT

James ended this discussion of controlling the tongue and of living by God's wisdom instead of worldly, fake wisdom by noting the legacy of a life lived in humility before God. What is the effect of living by God's wisdom?

Check out James 3:18 to find out. Write down your own paraphrase in the space provided.

Whew! That's a lot of churchy words in one verse. Here's another way to look at it: godly wisdom creates a cycle of righteousness (right living) that flourishes and grows in a peaceful setting—peace between God and His people and peace between people themselves. **As a follower of Jesus, your life will bear the fruit of peace.**

✳ Evaluate your life. Does it show the fruit of God's wisdom? Can people see peace? Can people see that you do what is right and what is just? Take a few minutes to reflect on these things. Journal about what God is saying to you about what you've learned today.

TRAINING MANUAL

Today, you'll read James 5. Use the following outline to help guide your interaction with Scripture as the Holy Spirit speaks to you.

* Pray.

* Read the entire chapter.

* What is God telling you about Himself in these verses? Notice anything different the Holy Spirit brought to mind today?

* Paraphrase the major points of James 5:

* What is God telling you about yourself and/or others in this passage? How does it compare to what you've written in previous weeks (pp. 33, 60, 87, 114)?

* What steps will you take to respond to what God has taught you today?

* What steps will you take to respond to what God has revealed to you in these verses?

✳ Faith Under Pressure: Humble

My husband is a huge University of Alabama fan. He's been one since he was 7 years old and went to his first football game, during which Alabama absolutely crushed its opponent (that'll leave an impression on a young boy). He has countless Alabama shirts and at least a dozen hats with the unmistakable *A* somewhere on them. One of the phones in our house plays the Alabama fight song as its ringer. His loyalty runs deep.

That is until Alabama plays his alma mater, Middle Tennessee State University. It has only happened once that I can remember, but I remember it well. We went to that game. And my husband was deeply troubled. Should he root for the school that gave him his education? Or should he cheer for the team that he has followed since before he really understood the game or the stakes? Even his clothes seemed divided over the issue: he wore a T-shirt from Alabama and a hat from MTSU.

My husband stayed neutral as long as he could. His heart gave way, and he chose a side. He couldn't stand divided loyalties.

This week, you'll learn about loyalties. And just like my husband, you'll learn that divided loyalties will destroy you. You must choose a side.

It's not about you.

The date: May 1, 2011
The place: Rochester Institute of Technology
The event: The largest game of dodgeball ever played

An astounding 2,136 players split into two teams—orange and brown—and gathered in a 60,000 square-foot field house in a battle for the ages. A sea of college students and faculty ebbed and flowed back and forth as players hurled 650 dodge balls across the room. More than an hour later, the final player on the brown team was defeated in the battle.[1]

Some fights would be fun to watch. (You can even watch that epic dodgeball battle on YouTube.) Others are not so fun to watch. Arguments between husband and wife. Fights between brother and sister. Locker room brawls.

The worst? A fight between two friends, especially when both want you to take their side. No one likes to be in the middle of one of those fights.

This week, you'll be digging into the fourth chapter of James. In it, he warns his church about the damaging consequences of a self-centered and self-serving life. Unfortunately, one of the outcomes is broken relationships.

Read James 4:1-3 and answer the questions in the next column.

* Who are the people described here?

* According to this passage, what is the cause of these fights and quarrels?

* Is there a difference between fights and quarrels? Explain.

* According to the verses, what did the people do to get what they wanted?

* What did James say was the reason for unanswered prayer?

* What does it mean to covet? Why is coveting such a big deal?

✻ THE GUILTY CULPRITS

Let's dig a little deeper into this chapter with a short review. Remember where we left off?

Time for a little review. What was the last verse of chapter 3 about?

Chapter 3 closed with a reminder that a life lived in God's wisdom would result in peace. This chapter continues in that vein (remember, James' original letter didn't have those nifty chapter breaks and subtitles), showing the people what kind of life results when someone chooses NOT to live under God's leadership and wisdom.

Keep in mind that these people were believers. Yet, right there in James 4:1, James describes the fighting he's taking issue with as "among you." Among whom? Christians.

Unfortunately, Christians are not immune to disagreements. Instead, they're a natural part of doing life together as a community of faith. However, that's not exactly what James was talking about.

The words "wars" and "fights" actually have two different meanings. Think of a fight as a long-term, ongoing serious dispute; on the other hand, a "fight" refers to one specific skirmish. Both are a reference to what happens between two people when there is major unrest.

✻ What is one long-term, ongoing conflict that you have with someone right now (maybe you're not even talking to each other)?

✻ What was the last short-term fight you had?

✻ THE SOURCE OF ALL THE TROUBLE

James explained the reasons behind "the wars and the fights." The source of the trouble wasn't philosophical differences or cultural mores; rather, the culprit is the "cravings that are at war within you" (v. 1). The word "cravings" doesn't refer to a hankering for chocolate when you have PMS or that irresistible urge for chili-cheese fries when you smell them at a football game. The word actually means personal pleasure, gratification, or enjoyment. It's figuratively used to refer to desire or lust. Get the connotation? It's not good.

✻ The reason for fights and quarrels is your own

———————————————————————————

✻ What sinful lusts or desires battle within you? List a few of them below.

When you take God out of the equation, you no longer live by His wisdom and will but by your own. You no longer desire to serve Him. And on your own, you're sunk. The result? Sinful desires that wage a war in your heart. And the result isn't good.

✳ WHAT DESIRES LEAD TO

According to verse 2, several things happen when you pursue your own path.

One paraphrase lays out the consequences:

> "You lust for what you don't have and are willing to kill to get it. You want what isn't yours and will risk violence to get your hands on it."
> —James 4:2, The Message

Wow! James seems over the top here, doesn't he? Maybe. Or maybe he was just remembering what Jesus said about violence.

Read Matthew 5:21-24 and reflect on Jesus' words. Summarize what you think He was trying to say in the space below.

These verses take place within the Sermon on the Mount (Matt. 5–7), the first words that Jesus ever spoke to a large crowd. It outlines right behavior for the people of God who have been transformed by His love. His followers are salt and light, honor marriage, love their enemies, give without expecting anything in return, pray and fast out of love and not just for show, and seek God's kingdom instead of their own desires.

In this middle of the best sermon ever preached, Jesus said, in essence, "You know that murder is wrong. I'm here to tell you that being intensely angry and flying off the handle is just as bad. Words kill, too."

I'm pretty sure you've never killed anybody because you wanted her iPad (although it has probably happened somewhere by now). And you've not murdered your friend because you were jealous of her new car. On the other hand, I am willing to bet that you've been infuriated at your brother because he wouldn't give up the remote. Or you've given your parents the silent treatment because they wouldn't let you go on a date with your crush. Emotions got out of control because you didn't get what you wanted. That's what happens when you live by your own desires instead of submitting humbly to God's best for your life.

✳ To what lengths have you gone to get what you wanted, even though it might have hurt someone?

✳ Write about a time when your emotions went out of control because of unmet, self-centered desires?

✳ Whom have you hurt in the past because you wanted, but didn't get something?

✳ When has a fight or argument broken out because you and someone else had conflicting desires?

✱ I DARE YOU TO PRAY

James indicated that the people at odds with each other didn't get an answer to their prayers. Why wouldn't God answer their prayers? After all, doesn't God want to "give good things to those who ask Him" (Matt. 7:11)?

Not always.

My daughter asks me for lots of things. And I like to give her things. Recently, our glamour-girl-in-training went to a friend's house and played with a monster truck. She *loved* it. Played with that monster truck every chance she could. So a few days later, I stopped by the store and got her one of her own. Why? Because I love to do good things for her.

I don't always give her what she wants. She would eat ice cream at every meal if I let her. She would never go to sleep, take a bath, or brush her teeth. She would do what she wanted for as long as she wanted and whenever she wanted. She knows only her own desires. And I know the consequences of allowing her desires to go unchecked.

God knows the consequences of allowing your sinful desires to go unchecked, too.

In fact, that's why James said God didn't answer the peoples' prayers. James clearly states that they didn't get their requests because those requests were sinful, lustful, and self-centered. And God, as the ultimate Parent, will not allow sinful desires to go unchecked.

✳ Name a time when you prayed for something and God refused to grant your request. Looking back, were your desires selfish? How was God a good God in not giving you what you wanted?

Here's a good test: If you are at odds with someone, pray. If you can't pray in honesty and transparency before God, then something is probably wrong in your desires and motives.

Today we looked at a self-centered life outside the wisdom and the will of God. Tomorrow, we'll discover God's perspective on our lives.

1. Jacob Sachs, "The Day RIT Made History," Rochester Institute of Technology [online] 9 May 2011 [cited 8 July 2011]. Available from the Internet: *http://www.rit.edu/emcs/admissions/bca/blog/item/the-day-rit-made-history*.

TRAINING MANUAL

Today, you'll read James 1 again. Use the following outline to help guide your interaction with Scripture as the Holy Spirit speaks to you.

WEEK
6

* Pray.

* Read the entire chapter.

* What is God telling you about Himself in this chapter?

* Paraphrase the major points of this chapter James 1. This is the sixth time you've read this chapter in its entirety. What new things did God point out today?

* What is God telling you about yourself and/or others in these verses?

* What has God revealed to you in today's verses? What steps will you take to act on what He has shown you?

He is jealous for you.

Imagine for a moment that you have been in a relationship with a guy for about nine months. You've been friends for years, but you just now decided to take the next step and declare yourself a "couple." You're both Christians, go to the same church, and share the same values. You even have some of the same friends. What would be the worst thing he could do to hurt you?

Rank the following offenses below, with 1 being the least painful to 10 being the absolute most painful. There are 10 statements, so you'll use each number only once.

_____ Forgets to text you good-night after he gets home from your date

_____ Forgets your birthday

_____ Chooses a weekend at the lake with his buddies instead of a trip with your family

_____ Smiles at another girl

_____ Hooks up with another girl while you're out of town

_____ Lies to you

_____ Laughs at you when you do a belly flop in the swimming pool

_____ Refuses to go to the prom with you

_____ Takes another girl home after youth group one night

_____ Won't change his Facebook status to "in a relationship"

How does this quiz relate to the Book of James? After today's study, you'll know exactly how the two connect!

✳ JUST ONE WORD

Read James 4:4. In fact, just read the first word of the verse. What does James call the readers? What names would you and your friends use to mean the same kind of thing?

Ouch! That's painful. Of all the names I could be called, I hope I'm never called that. So why did James use such strong language that could easily offend? A couple of other verses might shed light on his mind-set.

✳ But before you read, look back at James 4:1-3 and summarize what James was trying to say. Keeping that in mind will help set the stage.

✳ Read Isaiah 54:5. Who is the husband, and who is the bride?

✳ Read Jeremiah 3:20. Again, who is the husband, and who is the bride? What did the bride do?

✳ Read Hosea 9:1. Identify God and the people in this passage. What had the people done?

✳ Read Deuteronomy 31:16. Summarize what God told Moses. What specific terms did He use to talk about the people's sin?

When James called the people "adulteresses" in verse 4, he was using an image that his original audience would have understood at once. That's because these Jewish Christians would have been very familiar with the Old Testament, in which God had repeatedly used the imagery of a husband and wife to demonstrate the intimacy of His relationship with the Jewish people. God did not view His people from a distance; He didn't watch over them from afar. He was as intimately involved and emotionally invested in them as a husband is in his wife.

So James' original readers would have understood the term, but why did James use that word at this point in his letter?

Remember, in the previous verses, James was talking about the desires that were waging war within the people and the church because they had chosen to live outside of God's will and wisdom. In effect, they were choosing the world's system and values, which were (and still are!) directly opposed to God's. And when they chose the god of this world and its idols of money, fame, sexual lust, power and greed, they wounded God's heart.

While the image doesn't carry as much impact for you because you've never been married, you can appreciate what it would feel like for someone to betray you. And that's how God felt. Betrayed. As one person wrote,

"... to disobey God is like breaking the marriage vow. It means that all sin is sin against love. It means that our relationship with God is not like the distant relationship of king and subject or master and slave, but like the intimate relationship of husband and wife. It means that when we sin, we break God's heart, as the heart of one partner in a marriage may be broken by the desertion of the other."[1]

Think about that concept for a moment. How do you feel knowing that your sin and your choosing other things over God breaks His heart like a person whose spouse cheats?

✱ YOU CAN'T PLAY FOR BOTH TEAMS

James made it very clear that each person must choose for herself whether or not she will seek God's ways or the world's. And he made it very clear that you must choose. You can't just stay neutral.

Read James 4:4 and complete the following:

✶ Friendship with the _____ means _____ toward God.

✶ Whoever wants to be the world's _____ becomes God's _____ .

✶ Why can't you love both? Why can't you pursue God and pursue things that this world values at the same time?

To answer that question, read James 4:5. In the space below, write down your best paraphrase of that verse.

Scholars struggle with this verse because it's hard to translate into English and because even though James mentions a Scripture that specifically says "the Spirit He caused to live in us yearns jealously," there isn't one that explicitly says that. That doesn't mean James was way off-base. He probably had in mind several verses in the Old Testament that allude to God being a jealous God.

Check out these verses and summarize what they say:

✶ Exodus 20:5

✶ Exodus 34:14

✶ Deuteronomy 32:16

✶ Zechariah 8:2

In today's culture, jealousy carries a negative connotation. But for God, it's different. He is the faithful Lover of your soul. When He is described as jealous in Scripture, it doesn't mean that He is envious. Instead, it means that He demands complete faithfulness to Him and exclusive worship. Nothing else is supposed to have first place in your life. God loves you with such a deep passion that He cannot bear another love to take a spot in your heart where He alone rightfully belongs.

Talk to God about His jealous love for you. How do you feel? What do you want to say in response? Take time to reflect, and then write your prayer below.

✳ THE POWER OF LOVE

Such powerful, intense, deep, and enduring love requires that you respond to Him in love and faithfulness. But how could we possibly love Him in a way that He wants to be loved and deserves to be loved?

Read James 4:6. How can you and I love God faithfully?

It's ironic. Not only does God love us intensely and passionately, but He provides the grace to walk in close fellowship with Him. He also knows that on our own, we'd chase after every god that our sinful appetites could find. So He provides the grace, the strength, and the ability to love Him wholly.

But there's a catch.

Read James 4:6 to find it. What is the one requirement for receiving God's grace to live as He desires?

Humility. God can't stand pride because when we're proud, we think we can manage life on our own, independent and free of God's direction. Pride keeps us from recognizing when we sin. Pride prevents us from recognizing that we are broken and wounded people in need of help.

So what does a humble person—that person who recognizes that she is lost and needs a relationship with God—do? Tomorrow's study will answer that question.

1. Wiliam Barclay, *The Letters of James and Peter*, (Louisville, Ky.: Westminster John Knox Press, 2003), 118.

TRAINING MANUAL

Today, you'll read James 2. Use the following outline to help guide your interaction with Scripture as the Holy Spirit speaks to you.

* Pray.

* Read the entire chapter.

* What is God telling you about Himself in this passage? This is the sixth time you've read this chapter during this study. What new things did God bring to light today?

* Paraphrase the major points of this chapter:

* What is God telling you about yourself and/or others in this passage?

* What steps will you take to respond to what God has revealed to you in this chapter?

Don't break His heart.

For most of his letter, James was addressing Christians. However, in today's portion of Scripture, he turns his focus and specifically speaks to the non-Christians in the church who might have been listening as the letter was read aloud. Based on chapter 2 of the letter, we can infer that there were some people in the church who claimed to be Christians but whose actions demonstrated otherwise.

It is to these people who had chosen the world over God that James wrote the words you are about to read.

To put you in the right frame of mind, picture yourself as an unbeliever for a moment. What are you pursuing? How do you feel when no one is around? What do you want out of your life? Are you happy or sad? You might even want to write about a non-Christian you know. Here's some space to jot down your thoughts:

James didn't mince words in talking to them. He wasn't concerned about anybody's feelings. He was more worried about the people hearing and responding to the truth!

Read James 4:7-10 and complete the following:

✳ What was the first thing James told the people to do? Why must that be the first step?

✳ Why did James mention resisting the Devil?

✳ In verses 8-10, what other sorts of things did James challenge his lost readers to do?

Yesterday you were challenged to present yourself humbly before God as one in need of grace. Verse 6 told us that God resists the proud but gives grace to the humble. Because God's grace is offered only to those who humbly admit their need, James' message was simple: **submit.** Voluntarily place yourself under God's authority and will. The girl who cannot submit herself to God is also the girl who cannot admit that she needs God. Unless you recognize that you need God, you'll never know His grace and forgiveness and will remain lost and without hope.

* When you hear the word, "submit," what emotions emerge in you? Do you struggle with submitting to God? Explain.

By the very definition of the word, submitting yourself to God naturally means resisting the Devil. The word "resist" literally means "to stand against" or "to oppose." This sounds a lot like what James said earlier in the chapter when he talked about choosing sides.

Go back to page 151 to recall what it means to choose to be a friend of God. Write your thoughts below:

The truth is, you can't embrace a relationship with God and constantly choose to sin.

✱ THE GOOD NEWS

James gave all of us a bit of good news in verse 7. What is it?

Believe it or not, the Devil is not all-powerful. He can be defeated. He cannot make you sin. In fact, based on Jesus' example in Matthew 4:1-11, when you draw near to God and rely on the truth of Scripture to respond to Satan's attacks, he will flee. This is probably what James had in mind in this verse.

* How does this understanding of the Devil differ from what our culture tells us? How is this picture of the Devil different than what you might have grown up believing?

✱ WHAT REPENTANCE LOOKS LIKE

In verses 8-10, James provided a vivid picture of what repentance looks like. He used several word groupings to make his point.

Read James 4:8-10 and complete the groupings:

Draw near to _____ and He will _____

_____.

_____ your hands and _____

your hearts. Be _____ and _____

and_____. Your laughter must _____

_____ and your joy to _____.

James' inner poet was coming out in these verses—and that isn't necessarily a weird thing. Hymn writers and poets of the day often cobbled couplets together into a verse or a song as a way to emphasize the point they were trying to make. (That's why some of the verses in Psalms seem to repeat each other.) It's quite possible that James simply relied on a tried-and-true method to make his case when he turned to poetry in these verses.

But James wasn't just writing a few pretty sentences in a letter. In telling the people to cleanse their hearts, James was making a reference to ceremonial washing done by priests in the Old Testament. The point James seems to be making here isn't about making sure you're outwardly clean. It's not about telling the people a list of things they need to do in order for God to accept them, because there's nothing you and I can do to earn God's favor or grace.

✳ So what do you think James was saying? What do "cleanse" and "purify' mean in this passage?

James was referring back to earlier verses. Read over the phrases he used in verse 7 and the early part of verse 8: *submit* yourself to God; *draw near* to God; *humbly turn back* to God. James was telling these people whom he loved to turn to God for cleansing. To stop trying to manage their own sin. To choose God. To ask God to do

what only He can do. Because James understood (like I hope you understand) that we can't save ourselves. Only when we look to Jesus can we be saved from our sin and its consequences. (Check out John 3:14-18 for more.)

✶ IT'S NO LAUGHING MATTER

Not only did James tell the people to draw near to God for cleansing, He also commanded them to do something else. **Look back at verse 9 and write what it was.**

Why would James tell anyone to be miserable? After all, isn't the message of forgiveness good news? Shouldn't James be telling the people to celebrate forgiveness instead of mourning and weeping?

Write your thoughts below:

When you read it at first glance, verse 9 makes James sound pretty depressing—head held low, dejected, and confused. But James wasn't depressed. He was just looking at his own sin with his eyes wide open.

When you realize that you have hurt someone, remorse is a natural reaction. You might cry. You'll feel miserable and upset. You might even mourn. Get the parallel? **Sin breaks God's heart.** Remember, He is the Lover of your soul who pursues you and yearns for you to return to Him and stop chasing the false lovers the world and our own sinfulness tell us are so important.

James' admonition to recognize our sinful condition before God and to weep in grief and remorse over our sin carries such significance in today's culture where "anything goes." You live in a world that says you can do whatever you want because it feels good for you. What's OK for you is OK.

Scripture makes it clear that sin is not OK. It damages your relationship with God and other people. It hinders you from being all that God created you to be. Sin always takes you further than you want to go. It always keeps you longer than you want to stay. And it always costs you more than you want to pay.

When you recognize the consequences of sin and the great lengths to which God went to rescue you, you can't help but weep and mourn.

✷ WHAT'S IT TO YOU?

You may be thinking to yourself, *I thought you just said that James was addressing non-Christians in these verses. I'm a Christian, so how do these verses relate to me?* Good question.

The answer depends on your behavior. How do you respond to sin in your own life? Do you laugh it off, thinking it's no big deal? Do you treat your relationship with God so lightly that you don't notice when you sin and hurt God?

Take some time to reflect on today's verses. Journal your response to God below.

TRAINING MANUAL

Today, you'll read James 3. Use the following outline to help guide your interaction with Scripture as the Holy Spirit speaks to you.

＊ Pray.

＊ Read the entire chapter.

＊ Paraphrase the major points of this chapter. What new things did the Holy Spirit teach you?

＊ What is God telling you about Himself in James 3?

＊ What is God telling you about yourself and/or others in these verses? How does that compare to what you've written in previous weeks? (See pp. 23, 51, 76, 103,131.)

＊ What specific actions will you take to respond to what God has shown you in these verses?

✳ *Arrogance with others*

Walk down the hall in any middle school or high school and you are likely to hear the following (or something like it):

"She's such a skank."

"Can you believe she wore that to school?"

"Did you hear what she did over the weekend?"

"She is so two-faced. You can't trust her."

Slander. It's a part of everyday life in today's culture. Because it's so easy to commit, it's almost impossible to escape its nasty claws—either as the offender or the victim. Slander seems especially rampant among girls and women, probably because we are, for the most part, more relationship-driven and more talkative than men.

With the rise of digital media and social media networks like Facebook, Twitter, and Formspring, slander takes place instantly, continually, and anonymously. However, the problem of slander is not new. In fact, God often spoke against slandering others in the Old Testament. (Check out Ps. 50:20; 101:5.) And James 4:11-12 tell us that slander was a problem in first century Jerusalem, too.

Read James 4:11-12. In the space provided below, write down all the words that you think are significant:

✳ AN ENGLISH LESSON

In today's Scripture passage, James told the church not to criticize each other. The word translated *criticize* here can be translated a lot of different ways. It can mean *to slander, bad-mouth, speak evil, accuse, speak against, backbite, say cruel things, gossip,* or *falsely accuse.* Do you get the picture James was painting? The original language carries with it the idea of a verbal attack toward a person who is not there to offer a defense. James was talking about vicious, unfair, behind-the-back attacks. The people in James' original audience weren't just offering constructive criticism to one another out of a spirit of love and a desire to help one another become more godly people. They were talking behind each other's backs and as the original language suggests, saying cruel things fueled by spiteful desires.

✳ ALL IN THE FAMILY

Did you notice that James used the word "brother" a lot in verse 11? Go back and count how many times he used it. I counted three times in one verse—and there are only 21 words in the sentence!

✳ Why do you think James emphasized the concept of family when talking about slander?

159

Scripture tells us to expect slander and unkind words from non-Christians (1 Pet. 2:12). However, slander is the opposite of what is expected and needed within the family of faith, which is exactly who James was writing to.

Read Ephesians 4:29-31. Jot down the words that describe the kind of speech that is supposed to characterize the church.

Fact is, we're all on the same team. For us to tear each other down and slander each other would be like one of your soccer teammates screaming "What a loser!" if you missed a goal. This kind of negative, mean-spirited talk just shouldn't happen among the followers of Christ. Our bonds as God's family are violated when we put each other down.

✳ JUDGING A BROTHER

James made some pretty interesting connections between criticism, judgment, and the law in today's verses.

Complete the following equation using verse 11 as your guide:

Judging a brother = _____ the law

Judging the law = setting yourself up as a _____ of the law

Judging someone (criticizing, slandering, saying cruel things about her) is the same as criticizing the law.

✳ What law was James talking about? Go back to James 2:8 to refresh your memory:

The royal law of love is this: love your neighbor as yourself. When you criticize this law of love, you are saying that there's something faulty with this law. You are saying that the command to love others is not important, that it's a bad law and not worth following.

✳ What's your reaction to reading those words?

✳ BECOMING THE JUDGE

When we choose to slander others, we're not just saying that the law is faulty or unimportant; we're also setting ourselves up as a judge of the law. That's what James was talking about in verse 11 when he introduced the idea of judging the law. Instead of thinking of ourselves as subjects or followers of the law, we put ourselves in the place of the lawmaker when we slander others. When you do so, you are assuming the right and authority to determine the standard by which someone will be judged.

To put it simply, when you criticize, slander, or gossip, you place yourself above the law of love. And when you do that, you're placing yourself above the One who created the law in the first place—God Almighty. In judging others, you are taking God's rightful place. The problem with that? God alone is the sovereign Ruler and Judge of all. Only He has the right to make and enforce any law, including the royal law of love.

✳ WHO ARE YOU?

In verse 12, James reminded the people of their proper stance before God as he continued this discussion.

Reread James 4:12 and write it in your own words below:

✳ Who is the only lawgiver and judge?

✳ Who is able to save and destroy you?

✳ Why does God alone retain the right to judge?

Check out the following verses that give you one reason. What do these all have in common?

1 Samuel 16:7

1 Kings 8:39

1 Chronicles 28:9

One of the reasons God alone has the right to judge is because He is the only One who knows the hearts of men and women. But that's not the only reason God is the rightful Judge. You can discover one more very important reason in Revelation 4:8.

Read Revelation 4:8. Jot down why God is the only rightful Judge below.

God is holy. Perfect. Without sin. Eternal. God is God. Everybody else is marred by sin.

✳ Based on what you've learned, how could you paraphrase James 4:12?

Learn this hard truth well: No human being has the right to judge or criticize. No one, not even you. That authority belongs to God alone.

✱ SO NOW WHAT?

One of my favorite stories in Scripture is an exchange between Jesus and a sinful woman. It's found in John 8:1-11.

Read John 8:1-11 and answer the following questions.

✳ Who were acting as judges and critics in this passage?

✳ Who was the object of their slander? Did she deserve what they were saying about her? Explain.

✳ How did Jesus respond to the woman?

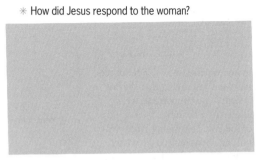

✳ What did Jesus tell the scribes and the Pharisees?

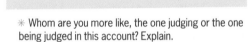

✳ Whom are you more like, the one judging or the one being judged in this account? Explain.

At one time or another, every one of us have played the role of the Pharisees, judging others for their sins without recognizing our own. Jesus' words to them also apply to us. If we don't have sin, we can judge others.

But the reality is that we're all like the sinful woman. We've all been caught in sin—and we're all guilty, every last one of us. Like the woman in this passage, we all sit at the feet of Jesus, broken, naked, ashamed, and in need of forgiveness. And the One who could have judged us harshly (and deservedly so) for our sin, chose to forgive and restore us instead. As Christ-followers, we should do the same, forgiving and restoring others rather than condemning them with our own judgment.

TRAINING MANUAL

Today, you'll read James 4. Use the following outline to help guide your interaction with Scripture as the Holy Spirit speaks to you.

* Pray, asking for the Holy Spirit's guidance and understanding as you read.

* Read the entire chapter.

* Paraphrase the major points of this chapter. Did you notice anything new in light of today's study?

* What is God telling you about Himself in these verses?

* What is God telling you about yourself and/or others in this passage?

* What has God revealed to you today? What specific steps will you take to respond to Him? List three below.

*

*

*

Humility and the future

Where do you hope to be in 10 years? What do you want your life to look like?

In the space provided here, either sketch a time line of what you want to take place over the next 10 years, or just write a detailed summary that tells what you hope will happen:

Someone once told me that between the ages of 18 and 22, we will make the most life-changing decisions in our lives. Think about it. Many of you are right there at this moment. You're making decisions about if you should go to college or join the workforce, where to go to college and why, what to study, who to date, if you should get married, join the military, or where you should live. So many decisions! Sometimes it's just so difficult to figure out the right decision.

✴ WHAT JAMES SAID

So, how *do* you know if a decision is the right one?

Check out Proverbs 3:5-6 to find out. Summarize what it says about making decisions:

Scripture talks about the futility of making decisions without seeking God's wisdom. James even talked about it. Today, we'll be diving into what he said about that and how it applies to our lives two centuries later.

Read James 4:13-14.

＊ To whom was James talking?

＊ What decisions were these people making? (Think about who, what, when, where, why, and how.)

＊ Why did James think this approach to life was wrong?

＊ In verse 14, what did James call these people (and us)?

✱ FOOLISH BUSINESSMEN

James was talking to a group of Jewish businessmen who had decided that they would go to another city, spend a year there, and make a profit. They knew what they would do, where they would do it, when they would do it, and why they would do it.

And they consulted God in how many of those decisions? That's right, none.

How much are you like them? While you may not be deciding to begin a start-up business in your local town, you may have already made lots of decisions without even thinking about what God would want. For instance, think about just 30 minutes in your school day—lunch. You probably spend that time without even thinking about how God might want you to spend it.

Complete this activity for a different perspective on that little window of time in your day.

	My Plan	God's Plan
Who (you eat with)		
What (you eat)		
Where (café, hallway, table)		
Why (what you accomplish)		

When I was in high school, lunch was a social event. It might be the same way in your school. In my school, you didn't want to sit with the social outcasts. You sat with your friends at the same table every day. And the goal was simple: catch up on the day, talk about teachers and classmates, and check out the cute guys.

Maybe you spend your lunchtime in much the same way. But what if God has something more for you? What if He wants you to sit with that new girl with no friends? What if He wants you to eat healthier foods? What if He wants you to sit at the table with the students who have special needs? What if He wants you to make a difference in someone's day instead of spreading gossip about the mean girl?

✱ WHY CONSULT GOD?

Close your eyes and concentrate on tomorrow. What do you know will happen? Jot it down here:

You might have written things like *go to school, do homework, go to the dentist, go to the game, go to church, eat dinner, talk to my friends,* or even *fight with my brother.*

But what truth did James present in verse 14?

That's right: you don't know what tomorrow will bring. You cannot predict what will happen in your life. It may bring great happiness—or great sorrow.

You need God's wisdom, perspective, and direction for the decisions you make today because you don't know even what tomorrow will bring to your life—or the lives of others. You may plan to sit with your friends, but unknown to you, that new girl is about to find out that her parents are getting a divorce, and she's going to need a new friend to make it through that crisis.

Or perhaps you obey God by sitting next to a new girl at church. She's quiet and shy but you become friends. What you didn't know in the beginning is that you're going to need her friendship in six months when you fall and break your foot, and she is the one who cheers you up the most.

Leaving God out of your plans is a bad idea because you don't know what all your tomorrows may bring. God does.

James provided another reason for humbly submitting your life to God. It's also found in verse 14. Write it below:

The answer? **Your life is vanishing like smoke.** Hopefully this verse doesn't discourage you. James wasn't trying to say that your life is meaningless like a puff of smoke, here today and gone instantly. Rather, he was trying to help you to understand that your life is short and frail, and because your life is like a grain of sand in the ocean of eternity, it would be foolish and unwise to plan it out and live it out without seeking God's will and purpose. **Simply put, James' message is: time is short, so spend it wisely. And the only way to live wisely is under God's guidance.**

✳ HOW TO APPROACH LIFE

The people who received James' letter had apparently ignored God's wisdom because they were choosing to leave Him out of their decisions. In essence, they were setting themselves up as the Ruler of their own lives. They had decided that they knew what was best and therefore didn't need God's input, wisdom, or guidance.

✳ If you met someone like that, how would you describe him or her? How would you feel about him or her?

To say you know what is best and don't need any help is the very definition of pride or arrogance.

✳ Remember James 4:6? What did James say God resists in that verse?

If God is opposed to pride, then the best approach to the future is to live in humility. That's the gist of what James was trying to say in verses 15-16.

✳ Based on those two verses, what might be a good question to ask God about your life, not just in big decisions about the future, but also in the little decisions, too?

Living in humility before God means that you and I continually ask God, "What do you want me to do?" If you ask that question and sit long enough to listen for God's answer, He'll give it.

※ Try it out! Listed below are some areas that might need God's wisdom and direction. For each of those situations, ask God what He wants you to do both right now and in the future. Then listen for His answers. Write down what He tells you.

Boyfriend/future husband

College

Friendship with _____

Career

Argument with _____

Relationship with parents

Money management

Spare time

✳ ONE LAST WARNING

James gave one last warning in today's Scripture passage. It's found in verse 17. Based on this passage about God's will, what is that warning?

So what is the "good" James was talking about? Ideas?

Answer: God's will. When God tells you to do something and you don't do it, you are sinning against God. You're rebelling against what He wants. That applies to the big things—like whom to marry or where to go to college—as well as the small things, like how you treat your parents or your sister.

※ To close your time with the Lord today, ask Him to show you areas where you already know His will but are choosing to disobey. Write a prayer of confession in the space provided.

TRAINING MANUAL

WEEK
6

Today, you'll read James 5. Use the following outline to help guide your interaction with Scripture as the Holy Spirit speaks to you.

✳ Pray.

✳ Read the entire chapter.

✳ What is God telling you about Himself in James 5?

✳ Paraphrase the major points of this chapter. What new things did you notice this week?

✳ What is God telling you about yourself and/or others in this chapter? Have your observations changed from what you noticed during the first week of this study (p. 33)?

✳ What has God said to you in these verses? What steps will you take to respond?

week seven

CONSTANT

Faith Under Pressure: Constant

I only remember experiencing true fear one time.

I was in college, driving home at the end of the spring semester. To most people, spring just means flowers, finals, and allergies. But if you live in Texas, it also means tornadoes—lots of them. And I happened to live in tornado alley.

As I was driving home, I began to notice that the clouds were becoming more and more ominous, so I turned on the radio. Soon, I heard those familiar words: "The National Weather Service has issued a tornado warning for…" and the voice went on to list every one of the counties I was driving through. *Great,* I thought. *Just my luck.*

And then it all happened. The skies darkened, and the wind kicked up. Rain and hail battered my car. I was in the middle of nowhere, driving an old clunker that was literally rocking back and forth from the force of the conditions outside. I was afraid for my life.

In that moment, I wasn't thinking about the latest music. I didn't care about whether my grades would turn out like I'd hoped. I was thinking about my family. My friends. My life. What my last words had been to others.

This week, you'll explore the things James thought were important enough to mention in the closing words of his letter. He wanted to make sure that these people he loved remembered some lasting truths—truths you need to remember, too.

Faith under fire

Your best friend texts you on your way to school.

Her: where r u?

You: 5 min from school

Her: Meet me @ my locker ASAP!!!! Gr8 news!!!!!

All the way to school, you try to think of what the good news could be. She already has a boyfriend. Her parents are cool. No drama that you know about. You get to her locker and she can barely contain herself!

"You remember that great aunt of mine who died? That one I didn't even know about?"

"Um, yeah, so . . . ?"

"We found out early this morning from some lawyer guy in California that she was like a bazillionaire. She never had any family but remembered that my dad treated her well at family stuff. So guess what she did? She left all of her money to us! We're like, rich!"

What happens to your friendship? What happens to your friend and her family? Do you think that being rich will be all she thought it would be?

How would you complete this story? Write your ending below.

There's no right or wrong way to end this story because there's nothing inherently wrong with money. Like fire, money can be good or bad, depending on how you use it. In today's Scripture, James begins the end of his letter by taking time to talk to some people who had obviously allowed money (and the pursuit of it) to take over their lives.

✱ PAY ATTENTION

Picture the setting of these verses as a classroom and James as the teacher. He's been talking to his students, then suddenly says, "Pay attention, those of you who think I didn't know you cheated on the last test!" (That's pretty much what his "Come now!" in v. 1 means.) These cheaters were non-Christian, wealthy people, but they weren't just any wealthy people.

Read James 5:1-6 to discover more about these wealthy people. Describe them here:

So why was James so angry with these wealthy people? What had they done? List the answers revealed in James 5:1-6 below.

✷ SELFISHNESS EXPOSED

Read James 5:2-3 again.

✷ What in the world do you think James is talking about in these verses?

James was actually giving us a little insight into first century life. People became wealthy in three primary ways: agriculture, clothing, and precious metals.

The term "ruined" used in verse 2 applied to the corn and grain. Think of it as food that has rotted before it could be eaten. The moth-eaten garments also described in verse 2 were probably outer garments that had become bug food because they had wasted away from lack of use. "Corrosion," used in verse 3, applied to impure metals left alone for long periods.

Did you see what all three had in common? These people were wealthy because they had crops, clothing, and precious metals—and they were hoarding them. These rich people kept everything to themselves, even though what they had could have been used to help others. They hoarded crops, and they were ruined. They didn't use their clothes, and moths ate them. They had silver and gold, but couldn't ever use it all, and it corroded. Scripture is very clear about God's distaste for those who ignore people in need. (See Amos 5:11-15, Matt. 25:31-46 for more on that.) James was exposing the selfishness of the rich people in the community. Money itself wasn't the problem; the problem was the peoples' attitude toward that money.

✷ THE METHOD MATTERS

James exposed the rich people not only for their selfishness, but also for the means by which they had gained their wealth.

Read James 5:4 and jot down the peoples' sin.

In first-century life, day laborers were extremely poor. They depended on a daily paycheck for survival. What they made every day fed and clothed their families. Without the day's pay, a man and his family would go hungry—literally. There were no crackers in the pantry or peanut butter in the cabinet. If a man didn't get paid, he and his family didn't eat.

Throughout Scripture, God has spoken in very clear terms against withholding payment from poor workers. (Check out Deut. 24:14-15 and Jer. 22:13 if you don't believe me.) Yet, as James pointed out in today's Scripture passage, these rich people simply refused to pay the poor what was owed to them. And the results were awful.

Read James 5:6. Below, record what happened to some of those poor people because they weren't paid what they were owed.

The situation of the poor people in James 5 was so dire that to deny them payment for any length of time would ensure their death. As one scholar put it when talking about this section of James 5, these people "die because they pour out their strength in their work, but the fruit of their work does not come back to them. They cannot regain their strength because the rich withhold their salaries."[1]

And the outcry of those poor peasants reached the very ears of God Almighty, whom James called the Lord of Hosts. Again, money itself wasn't the problem; the way it had been obtained was.

✳ HOW YOU SPEND MONEY

In James 5:5, James painted a very ugly picture of these unrighteous rich people. **Read that verse and create a picture that depicts what these people were doing with their money:**

The word "luxuriously" in verse 5 actually comes from a root word which means "to break down" and "describes the soft living which in the end saps and destroys a person's moral strength."[2] Let that sink in. That means that these very wealthy people were living extravagantly, self-indulgently, without any moral limits. The word *indulged* isn't any better. It carries the idea of plunging headlong into lusts without any shame or conscience. The idea here is that these rich people were spending their money however they wanted with no thought about what was right or wrong, or how their choices affected others. Again, the money was not the problem, but how they were using it was.

✳ THE END RESULT

So what did James have to say to these rich, self-indulgent, wage-withholding, luxury-seeking, future-ignoring people? That their judgment was certain.

Read James 5:1-6 one more time. List any words, phrases, verbs, or descriptions that give a hint about what would eventually happen to these oppressive rich people.

The cries of the poor for mercy and pity had reached the very ears of God. Because James knew that God would act on their behalf, he warned the rich to "weep and wail over the miseries that are coming on you" (v. 1). He told them that they had fattened themselves like cows greedily eating, but unaware of their coming fate. The day of slaughter—the day of judgment—was right around the corner. It was fast-approaching, inescapable, fatal, and final. As the scholar James McDonald put it: "Blind to heaven, deaf to warnings of hell, insensitive to the impending day of slaughter and judgment, the unrepentant, selfish, indulgent hoarders stumble blindly to their doom."[3]

Do you want that to describe you, too? I think not!

✳ SO WHAT?

So far, today's study has focused on some greedy people in history who faced God's judgment because of their ungodly, self-indulgent lifestyle. So what? How does that apply in your everyday life?

The same reasons the selfish people were found guilty are the same reasons you could be found guilty for the way you acquire and spend money.

Complete the activity below to evaluate your own life and see how these verses apply to you.

✳ 1. The people hoarded their resources when others could have used what they had. What resources do you keep to yourself that others could use? Think in terms of money,

property (computer, phone), possessions (car, clothes, etc.) or other things:

✳ 2. The rich exploited the poor in order to gain wealth. This is a lesson to learn: how you obtain money and possessions matters. What are some sinful ways you might get money? Whom might you hurt in order to gain money?

✳ 3. The rich spent their money in total self-indulgence. How do you use your money? Do you tithe? Do you give to charities? Do you help friends without expecting them to pay you back? Do you really need the things you buy? (How many pairs of shoes do you really need? How many songs are on your iPod?)

The lesson from this passage is a painful one. James was speaking to these rich people, but at the same time, he was warning early believers (and us) that we can easily fall into the trap of thinking that money is everything. Most of us live in luxury—at least in the eyes of other nations. The looming question is this: **What does God want you to do with what He's shown you today?**

1. Stulac, George M., *James: The IVP New Testament Commentary Series* (Downers Grove, Ill.: InterVarsity Press, 1993), 166.

2. Wiliam Barclay, *The Letters of James and Peter* (Louisville, Ky.: Westminster John Knox Press, 2003), 138.

3. John McArthur Jr., *James: The McArthur New Testament Commentary* (Chicago, Ill.: Moody Press, 1998), 249.

TRAINING MANUAL

Today, you'll read James 1. Use the following outline to help guide your interaction with Scripture as the Holy Spirit speaks to you.

* Pray.

* Read the entire chapter.

* Paraphrase the major points of this chapter. Notice any big differences from what you wrote last week (p. 148)?

* What is God telling you about Himself in this passage?

* What is God telling you about yourself and/or others in James 1? Did you notice anything different in light of today's study?

* What steps will you take today to follow through on what God has said to you in these verses?

✳ Hang On! It won't last forever.

What would you do in the following situations? **Finish each paragraph by writing your response:**

❋ You walk into the school and notice that a lot of people are looking at you. When you get to your locker, your best friend says, "You won't believe this, but Callie started a rumor that you hooked up with Jason over the weekend." You grab your books and . . .

❋ When you get home from school, you can tell something is wrong. Your dad is home. He never gets off work this early. You walk through the door and your parents ask you to join them in the living room. You can tell your mom has been crying. Your dad says, "You know I went to the doctor a while back because I've been feeling tired all the time. Well, the doctor ran some tests and got the results back. Honey, I have lung cancer. And it has spread." After talking with your parents, you go to your room and . . .

We live in a broken, fallen, cursed, sin-infected world. Trials and trouble and heartache are inevitable. Sometimes the trials come from situations, like cancer. Sometimes the trouble comes from a person, like Callie in the first example.

If you'll remember from yesterday, James talked about trials that came because of ungodly, wealthy people who were oppressing the poor. In the passage we'll study today, James shifted his focus from those wealthy people to the Christians who were suffering. In telling them how to respond to their situation, James also gave you and me a model to follow when we face suffering ourselves.

✳ YOU WANT ME TO WHAT?

Read James 5:7-11. Then focus on verse 7.

❋ What was James' practical advice for someone who is suffering?

Be Patient

Really, James? Be patient? Why not say, "Get angry!" or "Get revenge!" Because, honestly, when I'm struggling, being patient is the last thing I'd want to do, but it's the one thing that James instructed his readers to do. Why? James understood that it's easy to fall into temptation. (Remember that from the first chapter of James?) But being patient in suffering? When we're suffering, shouldn't we do something to hurry it along? Nope. Why not?

Why should we not hurry this process.
James 1:2-4

✳ REMEMBER THE END

Reread James 5:7-8.

✳ James provided a reason to have patience. What was it?

Coming of the LORD

James used a farming illustration of planting seeds and waiting for rain to remind his readers (many of whom would have been farmers) of the importance of patiently waiting for something to happen. But what were these believers waiting for? Jesus' return, that's what. James referenced the return of Christ three times in just two verses. This was a big deal to James, but why? The simple answer? James was reminding his church (and us) that our present situations are not permanent. They will not last forever. There will be an end to what we are enduring. Not only that, but when Jesus comes, He will bring justice.

Read James 5:9.

✳ What did James call Jesus in this verse?

The Judge

✳ Why does Jesus have the right to judge? Explain.

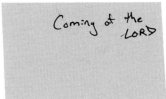
Judge our sins
Judge our lives
He is Perfect
He is Holy

✳ Why does James say Jesus is standing at the door? What does that mean?

✳ What do these verses have to do with your everyday life?

✳ When you picture Jesus as the judge, how do you feel? Explain.

James challenged us to endure patiently because 1) the situation won't last forever, and 2) Jesus will return as judge. He is perfect, and He is holy. He is the only One who retains the right to judge anyone. Remember all that you learned in James 2 about judging? It would be easy to fall into the temptation of judging (or complaining or arguing) in the middle of a trial (v. 9). But once again, James reminded us to leave judgment and justice to God. Even when you want to retaliate against someone, even when someone does the worst of horrible things to you, it's not your place to exact revenge or justice.

That belongs to God.

Obviously, James wasn't telling his fellow believers to stay in an abusive situation or to allow sin to go unchecked (we'll learn about that later in this chapter). God has established the justice system to bring criminals to accountability and to protect you and me. However, we are to work through those avenues, not *around* them.

✳ REMEMBER, YOU'RE NOT ALONE

James provided his readers with some concrete role models for us to follow—people who chose to walk with God in faithfulness and patience, even in the midst of the worst situations.

Reread James 5:10-11.

✳ Who were those two examples? _____ and _____.

✳ Read the Scriptures connected to each example. Summarize what you learn about them in the space provided.

Job	The Prophets
Job 1:6-22	Jeremiah 38:1-6
Job 2:10	Daniel 6
Job 19:25-27	1 Kings 19:1-3

James didn't go into detail about his examples because he knew his audience was well acquainted with the stories of Job and the prophets. However, we will stop and take an inventory of their lives because you might not be as familiar with these people as James' original audience was.

Job experienced the worst that Satan could throw at him, but he remained faithful to God. He persevered. So did the prophets. Jeremiah was jailed; Daniel was thrown into the den of lions; Elijah fled for his life. Scripture tells stories about people who persevered, who patiently trusted God and didn't waiver. And maybe the reason James alluded to these well-known stories of perseverance was because he knew they would encourage the people to whom he was writing. Such stories of perseverance can encourage you in your own situation, too.

✳ Think about modern-day faithful followers of God. Who are some people who have persevered in the midst of trials or trouble? Below, write about them, their stories, and how their perseverance has encouraged you:

✱ REMEMBER THE PROMISE

There's still one more little nugget of truth about trials to be found in today's Scripture passage. It's found in James 5:11.

✳ What is it?

_____

Somehow, some way, God will bring blessing out of the trials you face. Check out what happened to Job in Job 42:10-12. The last half of his life turned out better than the first half. Seriously. It makes no sense, but it's true. In God's kingdom, there is a blessing associated with endurance. It may not be something tangible, like great wealth or popularity. But you can trust that when trials come, blessings also come to those who endure—most notably the blessing of knowing God on a deeper level and becoming more like Him through trials.

✱ REMEMBER GOD'S CHARACTER

James saved the best for last—the best, most important thing to keep in mind when you're going through a trial.

✳ What final reminder did James give his church in James 5:11?

James reminded his original readers (and us!) that God is very compassionate and merciful. That's like saying the ocean is beautiful. Really, the ocean is beyond words, but you use words to describe it. The same applies to God. God is more compassionate and merciful than you and I can imagine. There are no words to really describe Him. It may be through trials and endurance that God proves He is compassionate and merciful—and He may cultivate the same qualities (mercy and compassion) in our lives through trial and endurance.

✱ WHY DOES GOD'S CHARACTER MATTER?

When you face trials and struggles, when you're at the end of your strength and perseverance, you'll be tempted to question God's character. _Does God really love me? If He really cared, He would take this away! Where is God when it hurts? Why is God doing this to me?_ Sound familiar?

In those moments when you're blinded by pain and overwhelmed by trials, remember God's character. Never judge God's character by your circumstances—they don't give you the clear picture (like viewing something through a smudged glass). God never changes. His character never changes. Let the truth of His character shape how you view your circumstances. He will come through for you. Always.

TRAINING MANUAL

Today, you'll read James 2. Use the following outline to help guide your interaction with Scripture as the Holy Spirit speaks to you.

* Pray.

* Read the entire chapter.

* What is God telling you about Himself in this passage?

* Paraphrase the major points of James 2. Look back through what you wrote in Week 5 (p. 126). What's changed?

* What is God telling you about yourself and/or others in these verses?

* How have these verses convicted or challenged you today? What specific steps will you take today to respond to what God has said?

I promise.

I promise I will keep my room clean from now on if you let me spend the night at Kara's house tomorrow night.

I promise to love, honor, and cherish you in sickness and in health, in poverty and in wealth, in good times and bad, as long as we both shall live.

I promise this won't hurt a bit.

I swear that the testimony I am about to give is the truth, the whole truth, and nothing but the truth, so help me God.

I promise I won't tell anyone.

✳ Which of these promises are you most likely to believe? Why?

At this point in James' letter to early Christians, he was beginning his closing thoughts. And what did he chose to close with? That's right, making oaths or promises. That James would mention oaths when he could have talked about a gazillion other things, tells us how important this topic was then—and still is today.

✳ WHAT IS IT?

✳ Read James 5:12 and summarize it below.

✳ So what is an oath? Grab a dictionary (or your phone) and look up the words "oath" and "promise." How are the definitions different? How are they similar?

What is an oath? Are oaths really necessary? Why would James make such a big deal out of them?

The concept of an oath was very familiar in biblical times. They were "statements by which a person promises or guarantees that a vow will be kept or that a statement is, in fact, true."[1] In the Old Testament, the name of God was used to show that He would guarantee the truthfulness and would bring discipline or punishment to the person if he or she lied. Just like today, oaths were often demonstrated visually by the raising of a hand. Sometimes oaths were sealed by placing a hand under a person's thigh. (Gross! I'm really glad *that* custom isn't still practiced today!)

But why are promises and oaths necessary? Because we live in a world that is controlled by the father of lies (John 8:44). Because we are a fallen people who are prone to sin, it makes sense that oaths would be necessary to hold people accountable to the truth.

✳ ARE THEY WRONG?

So was James telling us not to make vows at our wedding or to swear an oath in court? No. James understood that oaths were necessary under some conditions (like in court). In fact, when Jesus was taken to Caiphas before His crucifixion, He was placed under oath (Matt. 26:63-64). What James was protesting in verse 12 was the way his audience was using oaths.

Read James 5:12 again.

  ✳ What things did James tell the people NOT to swear by? Why would that matter?

By the time Jesus came on the scene, the religious elders (the scribes and Pharisees) had created an oral tradition that stated that only those oaths that used the name of God (*May God do so to me and worse if . . .*) were actually binding. They believed God wasn't involved in (and didn't care about) any other promise. So if they said, "I vow under heaven" or "I promise by my father's grave," they could go back on their word. Basically, this oral tradition created a loophole that allowed them to weasel out of an uncomfortable situation.

  ✳ How do people weasel their way out of their promises today?

✳ THE REMEDY

James was actually quoting Jesus when he told the people not to swear useless oaths.

Check out Matthew 5:33-37.

  ✳ What was Jesus' response to the old saying about oaths in these verses?

  ✳ What did Jesus mean by "Let your word 'yes' be 'yes,' and your 'no' be 'no'"? What would that look like in your everyday life?

  ✳ What did Jesus mean when He said "anything more than this is from the evil one"?

Jesus said these words in the Sermon on the Mount, during which He turned the Pharisees' oral tradition on its head. Jesus showed and told the people what God really wanted from them. Jesus carefully explained that swearing by heaven, earth, or anything else was irrelevant because God is over all and is involved in everything.

Instead of making oaths, Jesus told the people to just say "yes" or "no." In other words, a simple yes or no answer should be enough to convince someone of the truth. He wanted His followers to be so patently honest that there would be no need for an oath to back up their response. Fact is, the best guarantee that something is true is not an oath, but rather the character of the person who made the statement in the first place.

Think about a person you trust. Why do you trust her? That's easy. Because through her actions and her character, she has proven to be trustworthy.

On the flip side, think of someone you don't trust. Why don't you trust her? Because she showed herself to be a liar through her words, actions, and character. You can say "I promise," but if your actions don't match up with your words, people won't believe your words.

What about you? Can people trust you? Scattered below are several types of different people. How truthful would they say you are?

* Write down how each one of these people would grade you (A, B, C, D, or F).

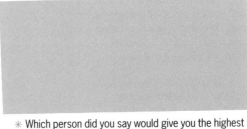

COACH _____

TEACHER

PARENTS _____

SISTER/ BROTHER

PASTOR _____

EMPLOYER

COWORKER _____

TEAMMATE

BEST FRIEND _____

CLASSMATE

ONLINE FRIEND _____

BOYFRIEND

* Look over those grades. Which person did you say would give you the lowest grade? Why? Explain your answer below.

* Which person did you say would give you the highest grade? How have you proven your trustworthiness (through your words, actions, and character) in that person's life?

✳ ONE LAST WORD

✳ What did James say at the very end of 5:12? What did he mean by "fall under judgment"?

James wasn't talking about God disciplining or judging believers. The word he used in the original language described God's judgment on those who have unrepentant and unredeemed hearts.

Those who continually and habitually lie as a lifestyle demonstrate that they haven't been transformed by God. Lying as a lifestyle reveals what's going on in your heart—rebellion against God. And a person in active rebellion against God and who rejects life through His Son will one day face God's judgment. James was once again illustrating that if you live a life of faith in Jesus, your actions will show it.

✳ Based on what you've learned today, what is God teaching you? Do your actions point to Christ? Why or why not? Are you trustworthy and honest? Is your life growing in the character of Christ as you develop a deeper relationship with Him? Why or why not?

Journal your thoughts and prayers as you answer these questions in the space below.

1. "Oaths," *Holman Illustrated Bible Dictionary* (Nashville, Tenn.: B&H Publishing, 2003), 1204.

TRAINING MANUAL

Today, you'll read James 3. Use the following outline to help guide your interaction with Scripture as the Holy Spirit speaks to you.

* Pray.

* Read the entire chapter.

* Paraphrase the major points of this chapter. Compare your paraphrase to the one you did during Week 1 of this study. What's different?

* What is God telling you about Himself in these verses?

* What is God telling you about yourself and/or others in James 3? How does that challenge you?

* What specific steps will you take to respond to what God has taught you in these verses? List three below.

    *

    *

    *

 Life together, part 1

Imagine for a moment that you are about to graduate from high school. Very soon you'll be moving into a new phase of life. For the last six years, you have been a part of a strong youth group, and now, as a graduating senior, you have a chance to speak to them and the incoming students. You have one final chance to encourage them and to tell them how to survive and thrive in their Christian faith during these years. What would you say to them? How would you encourage them?

List, describe, or even draw the most important things you would say:

James wasn't graduating from high school when he wrote the verses we'll focus on today, but he was ending his letter to a church he dearly loved. In the last few verses, he shared the last bit of encouragement that was on his heart. Fortunately, we get to hear what he said to them and learn from his words.

✳ LOOK AT IT DIFFERENTLY

Unfortunately, this passage of Scripture is often the topic of debate because of the emphasis on praying for the sick and what that might mean. True, this passage talks a lot about prayer, but it also gives us a clue about what life should be like when we're a part of a community of faith. So when you read these verses, try to look at them through a different lens, more wide-angle (focusing on the big-picture relationship with God and others) and less telephoto (focusing specifically on prayer).

✳ Read James 5:13-16. In the space provided below, list all of the different commands that James gave the church in these verses.

In these final verses, James told the people to pray. He told them to sing praises. He told them to call for the elders, and he told the elders to pray and anoint the suffering. He told the people he loved to confess their sins to each other. Finally, he told them to restore each other, which we'll study tomorrow. For now, let's dig deeper into the role prayer plays in our relationship with God both personally and as a community of faith.

✳ RELATIONSHIP WITH GOD

James obviously thought prayer was a critical aspect of communion with God and community with others. He used the word (or a variation of it) six times in four verses. But what is prayer?

How would you define the word prayer? What does it mean? Write your thoughts below.

✳ Think about the people to whom James wrote his letter. Do you remember their life situation? What was it? (Go back to Week 1, Days 3 and 4 if you need a refresher.)

✳ Why would their situation call for prayer?

A good friend of mine once told me, "Prayer is relationship." That is so true! Prayer is opening the door for conversation with God in order to cultivate a deeper relationship with Him. It allows God into your circumstances and reminds you that He is Emmanuel—with you in every situation you face.

✳ If prayer is relationship, then why would the persecuted believers James was writing to need to focus on their relationship with God in the middle of their trials?

✳ If prayer is relationship, then why would James tell the believers who were "cheerful" to pray?

✳ If prayer is relationship, why would James tell the sick and weak believers to call for the elders to pray?

✳ If prayer is relationship, why does confessing sin matter?

✳ If prayer is relationship, why is the prayer of a righteous person "powerful"?

Seeing prayer as relationship creates a whole new way of looking at things. In a trial, you're tempted to doubt God. But praying keeps that relationship in perspective and reminds you that God hasn't abandoned you. In the good times, you might be tempted to ignore your relationship with God, so prayer grounds you to the Source of your joy.

If you are struggling and weak, then it's harder to pray. The elders (think mentors and role models in the church) can encourage and strengthen your relationship with God when you don't have it in yourself to try. If you're rebelling against God, sin hurts your relationship with Him. So confession (admitting you were wrong) tears down the walls between you and God.

So what does prayer actually accomplish? Read verse 16 to find the answer. Concentrate on the last sentence of that verse. Write it in your own words here:

Scripture says "the urgent request of a righteous person is very powerful." Powerful to do what? James doesn't say. But if prayer deepens my relationship with God and my relationships with others, then something powerful must happen in those two areas of my life when I pray.

God does some amazing things in your walk with Him when you pray (or keep praying, as the original language suggests). It makes sense; the more you talk

to a friend, the closer you can become. And when you pray together about something or someone within the community of faith, something unique and powerful happens. Sometimes the situation changes. Sometimes it stays the same, but the community changes. Both are powerful transformations.

✱ WHY TALK ABOUT ELIJAH?

Read James 5:16-17. How does this story about Elijah fit in with the rest of James' final instructions? How does his story encourage you?

It seems rather strange that James would include this random illustration about Elijah (whose story you can check out in 1 Kings 17–18). Why mention him when talking about prayer?

The answer? Elijah was just like you and me. He doubted. He questioned. He whined and complained to God. (See 1 Kings 19 to see the whining and complaining in action.) Yet, he was a mighty man of God and a powerful prophet. What was the key to that? He prayed.

Whenever you read about Elijah in Scripture, you'll see him praying.

You're no different than Elijah. You're not perfect. You doubt; you question. You whine at times. But you can still be a powerful, strong, influential woman of God. The key? Prayer. The more you open up your heart to God and seek His will for your life, the closer you will become to Him. You will pray with power because your heart is aligned with His.

✱ RELATIONSHIP WITH OTHERS

Layered in his words of wisdom about prayer, James also said some powerful things about relationships with fellow believers.

Reread James 5:13-16 and look specifically for instances when James talked about the community of faith. Jot down what you learn:

In verse 14, James told "sick" Christians to ask for the elders' help. Sickness can refer to all types of weakness—physical, mental, and spiritual. Here, the reference seems to refer primarily to physical illness. In James 5:13, James had encouraged believers to share in the happiness of their individual praises to God; in verse 14, he stresses that the practice of praying for those who are sick must also be shared among the community of believers.

So what were these sick people to do? Ask for help from those who were stronger. That's what it means to be a part of a community—the strong lift up the weak. Two are better than one, after all (Eccl. 4:9-12). The elders would come to the sick one, anoint him or her with oil, and pray over the sick for healing. In today's Scripture passage, James invites believers to trust God with everything that affects our lives individually and as a community of believers, joys, sorrows, and sickness included.

✴ How do you feel knowing that you help the weak and sick by praying for them? Who are some of the weak or sick people in your church or community for whom you should be praying? List a few names below.

✴ What is something you've been struggling with? What has left you weak? Who can you ask to help you? Who can lift you up and encourage you? Spend some time in prayer asking God to reveal that person to you.

TRAINING MANUAL

Today, you'll read James 4. Use the following outline to help guide your interaction with Scripture as the Holy Spirit speaks to you.

* Pray.

* Read the entire chapter.

* What is God telling you about Himself in James 4?

* Paraphrase the major points of this chapter. Notice anything different in light of today's study?

* What is God telling you about yourself and/or others in this passage?

* What has God said to you about your life in these verses? How will you respond to Him?

☀ Life together, part 2

My mother-in-law and I drive the same interstate route to work. Every now and then, one of us will call the other on the way. The conversation will sound something like this:

"There's a wreck at White Bridge Road, so take the back way."

"There's a tree that's fallen at the bottom of the road (happens a lot when you live in the country), so drive carefully on the last hill."

"There's a police officer at the corner of Old Hickory and Highway 70."

We warn each other, protect each other, and help keep each other safe. Why? Because we love one another and care about what happens to each other. That's just what family members do.

In his final words to these early Christians, James reminded his readers of the importance of caring for each other, keeping each other on the right road, and not getting caught in a dangerous detour.

✱ WE'RE IN THIS TOGETHER

❋ Read James 5:19-20 and summarize what you discover in the space provided.

These verses tell us two things. First, when you become a Christian, you do not become immune to the lures of temptation and sin. James had already spoken about the power of sin and the reality of temptation. Remember when he said that an evil desire "gives birth to sin, and when sin is fully grown, it gives birth to death" (Jas. 1:15)? Temptation and sin can lead us away from our faith in Jesus and cause us to wander from the truth.

❋ Think about your own life. Have you ever experienced a time of wandering or straying from your relationship with God because of a particularly enticing sin in your life? What was it like to be away from the fellowship of God and the fellowship of other Christians? Write a few thoughts in the space below.

Second, these verses tell us that we're supposed to go after people when they stray from the truth. When a friend of yours stops going to church because she's head over heels in love with a guy and is sexually intimate with him, it's not OK to say, "Oh well, that was her choice." It's your job to go to her and tell her the hard truth that choosing a guy over God is a bad idea. Like warning my mother-in-law about a nasty wreck, you need to warn your friend that she's headed for a disaster of her own.

✱ BUT HOW?

In His grace, God gave us some guidelines for talking to someone who has wandered away from the truth.

Check out the following verses and write down what principles they provide.

✳ Matthew 18:15-17:

✳ Galatians 6:1-2:

Matthew recorded Jesus' instruction on restoring someone who has willfully rebelled against God. First, talk to her privately— don't confront her in the middle of youth group on Wednesday

night! Talk together. Help your friend see the danger in what she's pursuing. If she doesn't listen, then take another Christian friend from your church, not to gang up on her, but to show her the seriousness of her bad choices and to let her know you're not the only one who cares. If even that doesn't work, Matthew instructed us to take the issue to the church. (I'd talk to your youth pastor about it.)

In the end, if your friend doesn't change, are you supposed to ignore her? Is that what Jesus meant by let her be like "an unbeliever and a tax collector"? No! But the point is clear: you can't stay close friends with someone who is defiantly turning away from God in rebellion. Your lives are going in two different directions. You must love her, pray for her, and reach out to her, but you cannot share the deep intimacy of a close friendship because you don't share a common heart for God.

✳ Have you ever been in a friendship with a person who was actively rebelling against God? How did that affect your friendship with him or her?

Paul provided some insight in Galatians 6:1-2 about how to confront someone who has turned away from God.

Read Galatians 6:1-2. Write a few notes about what Paul cautioned believers or underline those phrases in your Bible.

First, Paul cautioned us to be gentle—to be fair, kind, and humble. Why? Because we're all prone to make mistakes. None of us is immune to temptation. If you approach a friend in arrogance or harshness, she probably won't listen to you or be moved to repentance.

Second, Paul warned you and me to be careful about being tempted. Tempted to do what? Well, that could be a number of things, like getting caught up in the same sin as your friend. Or Paul could be warning against pride or arrogance, thinking you are better than she is because you're not caught in that sin. He could be warning against judging that person. In any case, Paul knew there could be danger in reaching out to a friend who was caught in sin.

✳ BUT I CAN'T!

I know what you're thinking: *But what if I make her mad? What if she doesn't talk to me again?* I understand the fear. Nobody likes confrontation. None of us wants to be in that awkward position of telling someone else that he or she is wrong. But think about it this way: Would you want someone to warn you against buying a car that had faulty brakes? Of course you would! That's why you take a potential purchase to the local mechanic for a good once-over. Without knowing it, you could be driving a death machine, capable of killing not just you, but others, too.

Notice James 5:20.

✳ What does it say you would be saving by turning someone from their sin?

Answer: You are saving someone's life from death. Sin always leads to destruction. Without Jesus, sin leads to an eternity without Him. Even so-called Christians can find themselves facing death when they rebel against God—maybe physical death (doing drugs can kill you) and maybe spiritual death, if they don't know Jesus. You can endure a few minutes of discomfort and unease in confronting a friend when you know the price of keeping quiet—death.

You might also be thinking, *I can't confront her. I'm no better than she is. I'm a sinner, too.* What if you looked at it another way? What if you are the best person to talk to her because you are just like her? You're tempted, too. You struggle, too. The only difference between the two of you is your choice to rely on the truth and promises of Jesus. You can approach her in humility and let her know you're not perfect, but that you see something in her that really worries you. You don't want her to face the consequences of her sin. You don't want to see her hurt.

That's love.

✳ WE NEED EACH OTHER

Put yourself in the place of first-century Christians to whom James first addressed this letter. As a first century Christian, believing in Jesus could cost you your job, your family, and even your life. What would you need to help you make it through? Church buildings wouldn't matter. A stellar preacher would be last on your list. Lots of money wouldn't be an issue (besides, they didn't have any!). What they had was each other.

And that's what they needed.

When you're struggling, you need someone who will get in your face (gently!), encourage you, challenge you, and keep you focused and moving in the right direction. You need someone who will point you back to the Truth and help you recognize the voice of the Enemy who is trying to lead you astray. You need someone who cares more about your spiritual health than being liked. That's a true friend.

✳ A GLANCE BACK IN THE MIRROR

Think about James' life and words and ministry. How are you like him? What traits are missing in your own life? Use this time (and the space below) to speak to the Lord about it.

James cared more about the spiritual health of others than about being liked. He was a man who was not afraid to tell his congregation the truth, even when it was painful. He encouraged and challenged them. He provided vision and kept his church moving in the right direction. He called people to live by the truth. He was deeply concerned about the spiritual health of the people in his sphere of influence. And that passion led him to do and say what was right, regardless of what people thought.

WEEK

7

Remember, when the Lord shows you something, don't walk away unchanged (Jas. 1:22-25).

TRAINING MANUAL

Today, you'll read James 5. Use the following outline to help guide your interaction with Scripture as the Holy Spirit speaks to you.

* Pray.

* Read the entire chapter.

* Paraphrase the major points of this chapter. What new things did the Holy Spirit bring to mind as you read today?

* What is God telling you about Himself in this passage?

* What is God telling you about yourself and/or others in James 5?

* What has God revealed to you in these verses? What steps will you take to respond in obedience?

THRIVING

❋Faith Under Pressure: Thriving

This week, your time with the Lord in the Book of James will be a little different. For the past seven weeks, you have been looking at James through a microscope, digging into the tiny details of each chapter in order to bring a deeper, richer meaning to some Scripture verses that you probably already knew. You may have even memorized some of them!

This week, you will be taking a look at the big picture rather than the small details.

Throughout this study, you have read a chapter of the Book of James each day and recorded any insights you learned. This week, you will be assimilating everything you learned into one place—the pages that follow. You will look back at what you learned in each chapter and put it all together here. This will allow you to review what you've learned and see the big picture of how God has worked in you through this study.

Most importantly, you will have the opportunity to thank God for all that He has done in your life. It has been an amazing journey.

Now, let's get started on these last few exciting days!

 # James 1

Today, you will be reflecting on James 1. Look back at all of the things you learned from this chapter of Scripture.

In the places provided, record what stood out to you in each day's reading.

＊ Week 1
Day 1
(page 13)

....

＊ Week 2
Day 1
(page 40)

....

＊ Week 3
Day 1
(page 67)

....

＊ Week 4
Day 1
(page 94)

....

＊ Week 5
Day 1
(page 121)

....

＊ Week 6
Day 1
(page 148)

....

＊ Week 7
Day 1
(page 175)

....

You also studied James 1 during Weeks 2 and 3 (pp. 34-87). Look back over the pages and take notice of how God spoke to you through His Word during those weeks. What did you underline or highlight? What truths did you come to understand? As you look over your work, what significant points stand out?

In the space provided, jot down your thoughts about anything specific that you highlighted, underlined, or found especially significant.

✸ REVIEW: JAMES 1

Now, take some time to journal about the topics you studied in James 1. How did God challenge you in these areas? What were some ways He softened your heart to His Truth during your study of James 1? What have you learned over these last few weeks? **Think about these things as you answer the following questions:**

✳ How did God speak to you about trials during the course of this study? How did James' instruction for us to "consider it great joy" when we encounter trials in life challenge or change you?

✳ How did God speak to you about temptation in James 1? How did studying this book of Scripture help you to know how to better respond to temptation?

✳ How did God speak to you about a faith that doesn't waver? Did you discover areas in your life where your faith in God was wavering? What steps are you taking to stand firm on His Truth and promises?

✳ How did
God speak to
you about His
character in
James 1?

✳ In Week 3,
you read James'
admonition that
we not just be
hearers of the
Truth, but also
doers. How do
you understand
that better now?
How has that
statement and
your study of it
challenged the
way you live?
What choices
are you making
every day to be
someone who
not only hears
the Truth, but
does it?

✳ What did you
learn about
true religions
in James 1?
What does your
speech have
to do with your
faith? When
you truthfully
evaluate your
own life, can
you say that
the signs of
authentic faith
are there?
Explain.

✱ PRAYER JOURNAL

Look over the last few pages and all the work you've just completed. Then take a few minutes to skim over James 1. Now it's time to take a few minutes to have a conversation with God. **You can journal or sketch your prayer in the space provided below.**

James 2

Today, you will be reflecting on James 2. Look back at all of the things you learned from this chapter.

In the places provided, record what stood out to you in each day's reading.

✳ Week 1
Day 2
(page 18)

....

✳ Week 2
Day 2
(page 45)

....

✳ Week 3
Day 2
(page 72)

....

✳ Week 4
Day 2
(page 99)

....

✳ Week 5
Day 2
(page 126)

....

✳ Week 6
Day 2
(page 153)

....

✳ Week 7
Day 2
(page 180)

....

WEEK

8

You also studied sections of James 2 in Week 3 and Week 4. Turn back to those pages (pp.61-114) and notice how God spoke to you during those weeks of study.

Record below anything specific that you highlighted, underlined, or found especially significant, along with your thoughts on the subject

✱ REVIEW: JAMES 2

Now, take some time to journal about the topics covered in James 2. How did God challenge you in these areas? What have you learned over these last few weeks? It's time to find out. Think about these things as you answer the following questions:

✱ Think about the Book of James as a whole. What common topics or themes emerged across all seven weeks? In which area did God challenge or change you the most?

✱ How did God speak to you about favoritism in James 2? Did you evaluate yourself and discover how you struggle with favoritism? How is God changing your heart in this area?

✳ How did God speak to you about loving other people, the royal law discussed in James 2:8? To whom do you need to show mercy? What steps are you taking to do so?

✳ How did God speak to you about faith and works in this chapter of James? What does it mean to say your faith is active? Could you describe yours that way? Why or why not?

✱ PRAYER JOURNAL

Look over the last few pages and all the work you've just completed and read over James 2 again in your Bible. Spend your last few minutes of Bible study today in prayer. You may even want to read James 2 aloud to God as a prayer, asking the Holy Spirit to reveal the ways your life and attitude needs to change. **You can journal or sketch your prayer in the space provided below.**

James 3

Today, you will be reflecting on James 1. Look back at all of the things you learned from this chapter of Scripture.

In the places provided, record what stood out to you in each day's reading.

✳ Week 1
Day 3
(page 23)

....

✳ Week 2
Day 3
(page 50)

....

✳ Week 3
Day 3
(page 77)

....

✳ Week 4
Day 3
(page 104)

....

✳ Week 5
Day 3
(page 131)

....

✳ Week 6
Day 3
(page 158)

....

✳ Week 7
Day 3
(page 185)

....

You also studied James 3 during Week 5 (pp. 115-141). Take some time right now to turn back to Week 5 and look over your work. Take note how God spoke to you during that week of the study.

In the space provided below, record below anything specific that you highlighted, underlined, or found especially significant:

✳ REVIEW: JAMES 3

Now, take some time to journal about the topics you studied in James 3. How did God challenge you in these areas? How did God change your mind, encourage, or convict you? Quickly read over James 3 one more time to refresh your memory about what it says, then answer the following questions:

✳ What are some of the big topics James discussed in James 3? If you think of the Book of James as a whole, how do these topics fit into the big picture?

✳ Looking at the Book of James in its entirety, what common topics or themes emerged? Why do you think James kept returning to these topics?

✳ How did
God speak
to you about
controlling your
tongue in James
3? How has your
speech changed
after studying
these verses?
What did you
learn about the
power of your
words in this
chapter?

✳ How did God
speak to you
about earthly
wisdom in these
verses? Are
you trusting in
earthly wisdom
or godly
wisdom? Explain.

✳ How is
godly wisdom
different from
earthly wisdom?
What does
godly wisdom
have to do with
depending on
God? How are
you depending
on God today?

✴ PRAYER JOURNAL

Look over the last few pages and all the work you've just completed. Open your Bible and skim over James 3 one more time, taking note of anything you underlined or circled in the text. Now, spend the next few minutes in conversation with God, the only One who can give you true wisdom and peace. **You can journal or sketch your prayer in the space provided.**

James 4

Today, you will be reflecting on James 4. Look back at all of the things you learned about this chapter.

In the places provided, record what you learned on that day.

✳ Week 1
  Day 4
  (page 28)

....

✳ Week 2
  Day 4
  (page 55)

....

✳ Week 3
  Day 4
  (page 82)

....

✳ Week 4
  Day 4
  (page 109)

....

✳ Week 5
  Day 4
  (page 136)

....

✳ Week 6
  Day 4
  (page 163)

....

✳ Week 7
  Day 4
  (page 190)

....

You also studied James 4 during Week 6. Take a few minutes and turn back to those pages pp. 142-168), noticing how and what God taught you during that week of study.

In the space below, record anything specific that you highlighted, underlined, or found especially significant:

✳ REVIEW: JAMES 4

Now, take some time to journal about the topics we covered during our study of James 4. How did God challenge you in those areas? What areas of disobedience or rebellion did He reveal? Think about these things as you answer the following questions:

✳ What did you learn about self-centered desires and unanswered prayers in these verses? Did God reveal any selfish desires in your heart that were keeping you from desiring (and getting!) the better things He wanted for you?

✳ What did God teach you about friendship with the world? Are you seeking God's ways or the world's? How do you know?

WEEK

8

✳ How did
God speak to
you about your
humility toward
Him (or lack of
it)? How did His
prodding in that
area change the
way you acted
toward Him?
Explain.

✳ How did God
speak to you
about criticism?
Did you realize
that criticism
is a problem
for you? Why or
why not? What
changed in your
life or attitude
as a result of
studying this
topic?

✳ PRAYER JOURNAL

Look over the last few pages and all the work you've just completed. Take a few minutes to read over James 4 in your Bible one last time. Now, spend the last few minutes of your Bible study time talking with God. Focus your prayer on the things God has taught you in James 4. **You can journal or sketch your prayer in the space provided below.**

 *James 5*

 WEEK 8

Today, you will be reflecting on James 5. Look back at all of the things you learned about this chapter.

In the spaces provided below, record what you learned on that day.

❋ Week 1
Day 5
(page 33)

....

❋ Week 2
Day 5
(page 45)

....

❋ Week 3
Day 5
(page 87)

....

❋ Week 4
Day 5
(page 114)

....

❋ Week 5
Day 5
(page 141)

....

❋ Week 6
Day 5
(page 167)

....

❋ Week 7
Day 5
(page 195)

....

You studied James 5 more deeply in Week 7 (pp. 169-195). Take a few minutes right now and turn back to those pages. Take notice of the things you underlined, circled, or wrote in big letters. What did God teach you during this week of study?

Record below anything specific that you highlighted, underlined, or found especially significant:

✷ REVIEW: JAMES 5

Now, take some time to journal about the topics you studied in James 5. How did God challenge you in those areas? How did He change your way of thinking? Did He encourage or convict you? What have you learned and how has it affected your life? Think about these things as you answer the following questions:

✷ Think about the Book of James as a whole. What are some of the common themes in this Book of Scripture? Which ones appeared in James 5? What new things did you learn about them in this chapter?

✷ What did God teach you about selfish wealth and how you spend or use your money? What changes did you make in this area because of God's words in James 5?

✳ What did you learn about endurance in these verses? In what areas of your life do you believe God is calling you to endure as you follow Him?

✳ What did God teach you about honesty in James 5? What realizations did you have about this topic? How did what you learned change the way you live your everyday life?

✳ How did God speak to you about prayer? What did you learn about prayer and its important role within the community of believers? How did the verses on prayer challenge or encourage you?

✳ PRAYER JOURNAL

Open your Bible to James 5 and read over it quickly, then take a few minutes to look over the last few pages and all the work you've just completed. Concentrate on what you've learned and what God has taught you throughout this study. Spend a few moments quieting yourself before God, then spend the last bit of your Bible study time in prayer. Focus your prayer on the things God has taught you in James 5. **You can journal or sketch your prayer in the space provided below.**

☀ Introductory Session

This gathering provides a time for you to meet with the girls, distribute and review the books, and gauge girls' current understanding and knowledge of the Book of James.

WHAT TO BRING:

- Copies of *James: Faith Under Pressure*, one per girl
- Paper (for contact information)
- Pens

SETTING:

Host this session (and the following small group times) in a relaxed atmosphere, such as a home or a coffee shop. If hosting at home, provide snacks and drinks or ask girls to bring them. You may want to set up a weekly schedule so that each girl gets a turn to bring snacks and knows when she's expected to do so.

WHAT TO DO:

Distribute books. Encourage girls to write their names inside the front cover or on the front (so they won't get them mixed up!). Allow girls some time to thumb through the books and get a feel for this study. You may want to point out the introduction to the study on page 5 and explain the common elements the girls will encounter during each week's work:

❶ **Daily reading of James.** Each day, the girls will be prompted to read a chapter from James. On Day 1 of every week, girls will read James 1; on Day 2, James 2, and so on. This will continue through the duration of the study. Explain to the girls that they should read the chapter for each day in light of the week's theme. For example, Week 1 discusses trials and temptations. For Day 3 of Week 1, then, the girls will read James 3 and should look for themes of trials and temptations in James 3.

❷ **Daily Bible study.** This study challenges girls to develop the daily discipline of spending time in God's Word. The work is not difficult or time-consuming. It should take girls only 10-15 minutes to complete each day's work. If girls balk at the idea because they "don't have the time," challenge girls to sacrifice 15 minutes of texting or TV-watching in order to develop the most important relationship they could ever have.

WHAT TO EXPLAIN:

Explain that each week, you will meet together as a group to discuss how God spoke to you during that week's study. You will not introduce new Scripture at these small group meetings, but rather highlight the verses you and the girls have already studied during the week. These small group meetings will also provide time for girls to ask questions, dig deeper into Scripture, and talk about areas in which they are struggling.

WHAT TO REQUIRE:

Set some ground rules for the group meetings. Explain them clearly at the first meeting. Here are a few suggestions:
❶ **Keep things confidential.** The group will not share with others outside the group what is discussed during weekly meetings. This includes prayer requests.

2 **Be honest with each other.** Part of being in the body of Christ is cultivating honesty and transparency (this includes you as the leader!). Explain that this time together is a safe place where girls can be themselves.

3 **Treat each other with respect.** This means that slams, hurtful words, snide remarks, and hurtful sarcasm will not be tolerated.

4 **Commit to this group.** This means that girls will attend the weekly gatherings and do their homework. If girls aren't committed, it's likely they won't get as much out of the study.

WHERE TO BEGIN:

To gauge girls' understanding of the Book of James, administer the following true/false test. Distribute paper (or note cards) and pens. Read the following questions aloud and direct girls to record their answers on the sheets of paper or notecards. After you've asked all the questions, go back over them one by one, allowing the girls time to give their answers. Ask a few girls why they chose their answers and allow time for a short discussion. Be sure not to tell girls if they're right or wrong. Simply keep a mental note of their level of understanding.

1. The Book of James was written by the disciple James.
2. Trials and temptations are the same.
3. Religion that God says is pure and undefiled is obedience.
4. Faith alone saves a person.
5. God expects believers to do good works.
6. James was exiled to the island of Elba and lived there until his death.
7. Prayer is relationship.
8. When you rebel against God in huge ways, He turns His back on you until you repent.
9. James discouraged people from becoming teachers.
10. The perfect law of God does not bring freedom.

Just for your information, here are the answers: 1.) F, 2.) F, 3.) T, 4.) F, 5.) T, 6.) F, 7.) T, 8.) F, 9.) T, 10.) F

WHAT THEY WANT:

Close the time by asking girls to write on their paper (the back of the paper or note card they just used for the quiz) one thing they want God to do in their lives as they study James. Allow girls time to share their answers, then close with a time of prayer in which each girl voices her prayer to God. Close by voicing your own prayer about your own personal goals for this study, along with your hopes for the girls. Dismiss the girls, remind them to complete the first week's study of James before your next meeting.

OTHER SUGGESTIONS:

1 **Collect cell phone numbers and a parent's email address.** You can communicate with girls during the week using texting (they typically don't answer email) and communicate with parents via email.

2 **Create a Facebook group for your Bible study.** This will give you another avenue to communicate with girls. It will also give you a forum to ask questions during the week and to remind girls about their commitment to complete this study.

3 If the women in your church are studying *James: Mercy Triumphs* by Beth Moore as you are going through this study, you might be able to **borrow the DVD to use in your girls' group.** While each week's segments won't parallel each other exactly, you might find short clips from the DVD that would be useful in your small group time.

Faith Under Pressure: Possible

WHAT TO BRING:

- Notecards
- Pens
- Extra copies of *James: Faith Under Pressure* for any new girls

WHAT TO DO:

Play an opening game with girls to help them get to know each other better. Distribute the cards and pens and instruct girls to write two facts and one lie about themselves on their cards. Allow the girls a few minutes to think, then collect the cards and read the three statements. Girls will have to guess who the card belongs to AND which statement is a lie. The goal is for girls to remain "undiscovered" by thinking of truths about them that are not well-known.

Take a few minutes to explain the importance of getting to know each other as you journey together through the Book of James to the girls. Draw the parallel between the ice breaker activity you just completed and the material in Week 1, which focused on getting to know James, the author of the Book of James, as a person.

WHAT TO ASK:

Explain that each week, you will begin each meeting by asking the same two questions as you talk about what God did in the girls' lives through their study of James. To help girls understand what's expected of them, answer the following questions yourself first before asking the girls:

❶ **What was the most significant thing God said to you as you studied James this week?**

❷ **What is God asking you to do as a result?**

As girls answer these questions each week, **keep track of how God is moving in each girl's life** by jotting down a few notes about her answers. Write them down in a specific notebook or on the same sheet of paper. As the leader, you'll be holding girls accountable for what God says and asks of them during this study. These notes will help you fulfill that role.

WHAT TO DISCUSS:

Review the week by asking the following questions:

1. What did you learn about James, the writer of the book in the New Testament that bears his name? Why are those things significant to you?

2. Even though James didn't believe in Jesus until after His death and resurrection, God still used James in big ways. Why should that matter to you and me?

3. James called himself a slave. Would you ever want to call yourself that? Explain.

4. To what things are girls slaves?

5. What things are *your* master? *(See page 15 for review. Take time to discuss answers or any trends you see in the girls' responses.)*

6. What did you discover about the recipients of Jame's letter in this week's study? Why is any of that important?

7. What does it mean to you—if anything—to know that believers who lived long before you experienced the same struggles you do? Explain.

8. How do you feel knowing that you, along with believers who came before you and who will come after you, are a part of the same family and share in the same larger story in God's history?

If your church is studying *James: Mercy Triumphs* by Beth Moore and you found a clip that would be significant to girls, watch it together and discuss it afterward.

If you're looking for the answers to the quiz on page 29, they are: 1. B, 2. C, 3. D, 4. I, 5. J, 6. H, 7. E, 8. A, 9. F, 10. G.

If the girls in your group ask for the answers to the chart on page 31, please see the completed chart below:

Scripture Reference	Greek God	Roman God	Function
Acts 14:8-13	Zeus	Jupiter	king of the gods; ruler of sky/weather
Acts 19:23-28	Artemis	Diana	goddess of the hunt, wild animals, wilderness
Acts 28:11	Castor & Pollux	Castor & Pollux	patrons of sailors

HOW TO END:

Explain that each week, the girls will take turns praying in a closing prayer. Remind the group that the people James was writing to, the church in Jerusalem, met to pray, worship, and do life together and stress that this small group will do the same. If girls feel intimidated by praying aloud in front of others, encourage them to simply ask God to help each girl in the group to serve Him and Him alone and to turn away from other things that enslave them. **Share prayer requests and close in prayer.**

WHAT TO DO AFTERWARD:

❶ **Order more books** if necessary.

❷ **Contact girls this week via text or Facebook** and encourage them to follow through with the things God asked them to do this week as a result of their interaction with Him in James.

☀ Faith Under Pressure: Unwavering

WHAT TO BRING:

- Paper
- Markers
- Extra copies of *James: Faith Under Pressure*

WHAT TO DO:

Hand out paper and markers. Instruct girls to draw a picture that illustrates the worst day they had last week. If a girl(s) had a great week, let her illustrate that. Allow the girls time to work, then call for volunteers to share their stories. Be willing to share your own! **This activity will set the stage to talk about the main theme of this week's study: trials.** (Keep in mind that some of your girls may be going through major trials. Be willing to allow a time of discussion and prayer for those girls.)

WHAT TO ASK:

Remind girls that each week, you will be asking the same two questions as you talk about what God did in their lives through the past week's study of James—how He challenged, convicted, encouraged, and taught them. To help girls understand what's expected of them, answer the following questions yourself first before asking other girls (after this week, girls will go first):

❶ **What was the most significant thing God said to you as you studied James this week?**

❷ **What is God asking you to do as a result?**

Again, as girls answer these questions each week, keep track of how God is moving in their lives by recording the girls' answers. You'll be holding them accountable for what God says and asks of them. If a girl shares something she believes God has told her to do or stop doing, make a note of it and check back in with her periodically throughout the next few weeks to see how well she is keeping the commitment.

WHAT TO DISCUSS:

Review the week by asking the following questions:

1. On Day 1 of this week, you were asked to journal about a time when you faced a testing or trial of sorts (p. 39). What did you write about?

2. On Day 2, you learned about wisdom. Why is wisdom so critical in the midst of trials? Why can't you rely on your own wisdom?

3. Have you ever relied on your own wisdom rather than God's in a situation? What happened? What did you learn?

4. When you're going through a trial, what doubts do you typically have toward God?

5. On Day 2, you read about Jesus calming the storm (Matt. 14:22-33). On page 45, you also chose which character in that story you were most like—Peter in faith, Peter in his doubts, or the other disciples. Whom did you choose and why?

6. On Day 3, you learned about the crown of life. What was most significant for you in learning about this crown? Why?

7. Day 4 shifted to talk about temptation. What is the progression of temptation? What can it ultimately lead to?

8. How or when has God helped you to not give in to a temptation? What are some practical tips you can share of how to trust God and seek His strengths when you're tempted?

9. What temptations do you most often face when you're in the midst of a trial? (See pp. 54-55 for help.)

10. In the last day's study, you learned that God is good. How does God being the good and generous Giver help you in the midst of trials? Explain.

If your church is studying *James: Mercy Triumphs* by Beth Moore and you found a clip that would be significant to girls, watch it together and discuss it afterward.

HOW TO END:

Read aloud the last full paragraph in Day 5 (starting with "You may be reading this in complete disbelief…"). **Discuss why God's love matters in the midst of trials.** Explain to girls that no matter what they are going through, they can rest securely in God's love for them. You may want to allow a few minutes to discuss this truth and how it can have a life-altering impact on our lives when we truly choose to believe it and let God love us. **Share prayer requests, including any trials or temptations the girls in your group may be facing, and ask a volunteer to close in prayer.**

WHAT TO DO AFTERWARD:

❶ **Contact girls this week** and let them know you are praying for them in the midst of their trials and temptations.

❷ **If one of the girls is facing a major crisis** (death in the family, divorce, and so forth), communicate those needs to your church staff. They can begin to minister to the family as you seek to care for the girl.

WEEK 3

☀ Faith Under Pressure: Responsive

WHAT TO BRING:
- Stopwatch or watch to time Charades
- Paper
- Pens

WHAT TO DO:

Instruct girls to think about the most difficult thing they had to learn to do as a child (or something they are struggling with now). Allow the girls a few minutes to think about this question, instructing them not to share their comment just yet. After each of the girls has an answer, explain that you will be playing a short game of Charades. Each girl will have 30 seconds to act out her answer—without speaking. The other girls should try to guess what she is mimicking. Allow time for each girl to perform and instruct the girls to share the correct answer if no one guesses it. After the game is over, allow for a few minutes of discussion about why these things were so difficult to learn.

Use the game and the discussion following it to lead into an explanation that some of the truths from this week's Bible study are tough lessons to learn in the Christian life. Encourage the girls by admitting that they (and you!) may have wrestled with the truths in this week more than in previous weeks, and that's OK.

WHAT TO ASK:

Ask girls the following two questions, as in the previous weeks' debriefing. As always, as girls answer the questions, take note so that you can hold girls accountable for what God is doing in their lives:

❶ **What was the most significant thing God said to you as you studied James this week?**

❷ **What is God asking you to do as a result?**

WHAT TO DISCUSS:

Review the week by asking the following questions:

1. On Day 1, you learned about hearing and doing the Word of God. A person who hears but doesn't act is like what? (See p. 63.)

2. What does that mean? How did that truth challenge or change the way you lived your daily life? Explain.

3. After your study this week, how do you think we're supposed to look at God's Word? Why? Do you? Explain.

4. What did your pictures look like on page 65 (reflecting John 15:5-6)?

5. Who is someone you know who perseveres in God's Word? How does it show in that person's life?

6. What steps can you take right now to remain in Christ and persevere in reading His Word?

7. How can a law bring freedom? Explain your answer.

8. How does God's Word bring you and me freedom? (See p. 69, starting with the words "The Word saves us...)

9. Based on what you wrote on day 3 (p. 75), who are some people around you who are alone and vulnerable? What are some practical ways you can show Jesus' love, mercy, and compassion to them?

10. Day 4 might have been a tough day because it talked about favoritism. How would you define favoritism?

11. Based on what you circled on page 75 (Day 3), where are some of your areas of weakness in showing favoritism? What steps are you taking to deal with those areas of weakness? How can the girls in this group help to hold you accountable in those areas?

12. Why is favoritism a really bad thing to have in the church? Do you see any areas of favoritism in your church or youth group? What steps will you personally take to stop this trend in your life and your church?

To end this week's small group time, you may need to **have a serious discussion about favoritism** in your student ministry and even your girls' small groups. Cliques and favoritism are common problems among girls. Use the last few questions from the "What to Discuss" section to lead in to this conversation.

Talk about how others outside of your church, student ministry, and girls' ministry might feel about not being "in" at your church. If possible, prior to the session, enlist a girl to write a letter to your small group about how she feels as an "outsider" to the church or to the small group. This may be a huge eye-opener to girls who are clueless about how their actions, words, and behavior affects others.

To close this week's small group time, **direct the girls to spread out through the room or go to a quiet place in a nearby room,** if possible. The idea is that the girls are alone and won't have any distractions as they think and pray. Distribute paper and pens to each girl and instruct them to find a place where they can spend a few minutes evaluating the ways they show favoritism to others. Explain that the paper can be used to journal their thoughts or prayers and allow the girls time to confess any favoritism they might be harboring. Encourage them to think about how they can be merciful toward others because God has been so merciful toward them.

After a few minutes, call the girls back together in the same room. **Share prayer requests, including anything God revealed to the girls in the last few minutes, and ask a volunteer to close in prayer.**

WHAT TO DO AFTERWARD:

❶ **Write a note** (one you actually send in the mail!) to a girl(s) who may feel like she has been left out or marginalized by your youth ministry and/or church.

❷ **Send a text message to girls this week,** reminding them to be merciful toward others, not showing favoritism.

❸ **You will need extra preparation for next week's meeting.** Look ahead for what you need to do (p. 232).

WEEK 4

☀ Faith Under Pressure: Active

WHAT TO BRING:

• Words of wisdom (see "How to End" on the next page)
• Snacks that go together (peanut butter and chocolate, carrot sticks and dip, cookies and milk, etc.)

WHAT TO DO:

Prior to the session, **prepare several snacks with ingredients that just go well together.** (If you have prepared a schedule for girls to bring snacks for each week, make sure that you are signed up for this week.) Arrange the snacks carefully in a prominent place in the room. When you begin the session, **ask girls what all of the snacks have in common.** *(Answer: they are pairs that go together.)*

Use this activity to lead into a discussion about the focus of this week's study, which also dealt with two things that go together: faith and works.

WHAT TO ASK:

Ask girls the following two questions, as in previous weeks' debriefing. As always, as girls answer the questions, take notes so that you can truly hold girls accountable for what God is doing in their lives and what He has called them to do:

❶ **What was the most significant thing God said to you as you studied James this week?**

❷ **What is God asking you to do as a result?**

WHAT TO DISCUSS:

Review this week's Bible study by asking the following questions:

1. Based on what you wrote on Day 1 (p. 90), how would you define the word *faith*? What about *works*?

2. What is the relationship between faith and works for a believer? Explain.

3. What is the difference between saying you believe something and actually acting on it? What are some concrete examples of this idea that you can share?

4. On Day 2, you explored the idea of acting on your faith by helping people in need. On page 96, you wrote down the names and needs of some people you know personally. Without breaking confidentiality or embarrassing anyone, what are some of those needs? What specific steps can you (or our group) take to meet some of those needs?

5. What did James mean when he said that faith without works was dead and useless? Explain.

6. On Day 3, you asked God to "confirm your life of faith and works or to convict you that you show no evidence of a changed life" (p. 102). What did God say to you? (Girls may have questions, concerns, or anxiety about this. Make sure the girls know that they can talk with you privately after the session or at some other time if they need to talk more about what it means to truly be a Christ follower.)

7. On Day 4, you learned about Abraham's life of faith. Why is his story so important for you and me? How did it challenge, encourage, or convict you?

8. On Day 5, you connected the dots between faith and actions. What were some of the statements you completed in the activity on pages 112-113? How did this activity help you to understand what it means to put your beliefs into action?

9. What are some specific steps you are taking to put the things you believe into action in your life? How can our group hold you accountable in these things?

HOW TO END:

Prior to this week's group time, use social media to enlist godly adults to answer the following questions. You may want to use Facebook, Twitter, or even email to gather your answers. Prior to the session, write each answer on a separate sheet of paper. The questions are:

What would you tell teen girls about the fact that they were created by God?
What would you tell teen girls about their bodies being God's temple?
What would you tell teen girls about Satan and his desire to devour them (1 Pet. 5:8)?
What would you tell teen girls about the power of God's Word in their lives?

To close the Bible study, read the first question and distribute an answer (printed on separate pieces of paper) to each girl. Invite the girls to read their answers aloud, then allow them to discuss the wisdom that others shared. Repeat the process for the other three questions. Then, **challenge each of the girls to choose the most meaningful bit of wisdom they gleaned from this activity.** Encourage them to share that information and why they chose that nugget of truth.

To close this week's small group meeting, **instruct each girl to pray according to the piece of wisdom that she found most meaningful.** For example, a girl might ask God to help her live in the confidence as a girl created by God. Explain that each girl will have an opportunity to pray aloud during the prayer time. **Invite girls to share any additional prayer requests and close in prayer.**

WHAT TO DO AFTERWARD:

❶ **Make time this week to talk with girls who may be struggling with whether or not they are believers.** Questioning one's conversion is a common experience for teens, especially in middle school.

❷ **Write a note to girls who are living their faith out in real, tangible, obvious ways.** Encourage them in their obedience to make their faith known to others.

WEEK 5

☀ Faith Under Pressure: Mindful

WHAT TO BRING:

• Paper
• Pens
• Envelopes
• Stamps

WHAT TO DO:

Prior to the session, locate some old yearbooks (yes, your own!) and invite the girls to look through them. Allow the girls to make fun of the pictures and talk about how fashion and hairstyles have changed (thank goodness!). Take this opportunity to ask girls who some of their favorite teachers were/are and to share your own fun (or horror) stories of teachers you had in high school.

Use this discussion to segue into a discussion of this week's Bible study, which focused on teachers and those who speak wisdom into our lives. Get the girls thinking about this topic by asking them to think about and discuss people they trust to speak wisdom into their lives.

Ask girls the following two questions, just as you have in the previous weeks' debriefing. As always, as girls answer the questions, take notes so that you can pray for the girls—and hold them accountable for what God is doing in their lives:

❶ **What was the most significant thing God said to you as you studied James this week?**

❷ **What is God asking you to do as a result?**

WHAT TO DISCUSS:

Review the week by asking the following questions:

1. What did you learn about teachers in this week's Bible study?

2. Who are some people who look up to you? What are you teaching them?

3. Take some time to evaluate what you're teaching others. Don't just think about your words, but also consider your actions and every part of your life. Are you teaching them things that glorify God? Explain your evaluation of your life and any changes the Holy Spirit may be impressing you to make.

4. On Day 2 (p. 122), you completed the following sentence: Sticks and stones may break my bones, but words _____. How did you finish this statement? Explain your answer.

5. What did James say about the power of words? (See p. 124.) Why do you think he used such strong language? Explain.

6. Think about the following statements: *An action becomes a habit. A habit develops into your lifestyle. Your lifestyle defines your character. Your character determines your future.* Do you agree or disagree? Explain.

7. On Day 2, you wrote some notes about how certain types of speech could determine your character and your future. (See p. 125.) What did you write next to each? Why?

8. On Day 3, you learned that by the overflow of the heart, the mouth speaks. What does that mean? Why does it matter to you and me?

9. Now that you understand that your words come from the overflow of your heart, what do your words say your heart is filled with? Is that realization encouraging or convicting? If your words reflect a heart filled with anger, bitterness, and criticism, seek God. Ask Him to cleanse your heart and develop Christ's character in your life.

10. On Day 4, your study of James marked a shift in his letter to the church. He began to talk about wisdom again. Based on what you learned about wisdom, which kind of wisdom describes your life? (See p. 133.) Explain your answer.

11. What does it mean to completely depend on God? What does that look like in everyday life?

HOW TO END:

Distribute a piece of paper and a pen to each girl. Direct them to write a letter to someone (possibly a teacher) who has spoken words of encouragement and been a source of godly wisdom to them. In the letter, challenge girls to thank that person and to share how that person's life has influenced their own. Allow the girls several minutes to write their letters.

Direct girls to seal their letters in the envelopes provided and to write the recipients' first and last names on them. Challenge girls to find the addresses and mail their letters this week. Distribute stamps so girls won't have an excuse not to mail the letters!

To close the session, gather for a time of prayer. Share prayer requests and invite a volunteer to pray aloud. Encourage her to pray over the letters the girls have just written, thanking God for placing such wise, godly people in your lives and asking God to make you into wise, godly women who can do the same in others' lives.

WHAT TO DO AFTERWARD:

❶ **Write your own letter of encouragement and thanks** to a person who has been a source of godly wisdom in your life. Mail it!

❷ **Text the girls** this week to remind them to mail their letters.

WEEK 6

✳ Faith Under Pressure: Humble

WHAT TO BRING:

• Fortune cookies (These can purchased at most major grocery stores or ethnic stores.)

WHAT TO DO:

As girls arrive, point out the fortune cookies and allow them to munch on them. As they eat, encourage the girls to read aloud the "fortune" they found inside each cookie.

After several girls have read their fortunes aloud, **begin a discussion about whether the girls really follow the advice in things like fortune cookies.** Talk together about places or people from whom people in today's world often seek wisdom (things like mediums, horoscopes, other people, and so forth). Remind girls that part of their study this week involved wisdom and ask the girls where they most often seek wisdom. Don't just allow the so-called "Sunday School" answers!

WHAT TO ASK:

Ask girls the following two questions, as you have every time you've met. As girls answer the questions, remember to jot down a few notes so that you can hold girls accountable for what God is doing in their lives:

❶ **What was the most significant thing God said to you as you studied James this week?**

❷ **What is God asking you to do as a result?**

Take some time to look over the notes you've recorded over the last six weeks. How are the girls in your group growing in faith? Who do you need to check up on, challenge, or hold accountable for something God has asked of her?

Review the week by asking the following questions:

1. On the first day (p. 147), you wrote about a time when your emotions got out of control because you wanted something so badly. What did you learn from that experience?

2. How do you feel knowing that your sin and choosing other things over God breaks His heart, like a husband's heart breaks when his wife cheats on him?

3. What does it mean that God is jealous in His love for you?

4. James said friendship with the world is hostility to God. Are you a friend of the world? Explain your answer.

5. On Day 3, you learned about submission to God. When you hear the word *submit*, what emotions emerge? Do you ever struggle with submitting to God? Why or why not?

6. What do you think it looks like in our society to be a friend of God? Give examples.

7. How do you respond to sin in your own life? Do you think sin is something that can be easily laughed off, or do you consider sin a grave offense against God? Really evaluate your life; don't just give a Sunday School answer.

8. What is the "law of love" James talked about in James 4:11?

9. What's the big deal with a little slander, gossip, or criticism? What do they have to do with God's authority?

10. On day 5, you learned more about humility and the future. You created a time line on page 164. What do you want your life to look like in 10 years? Explain.

11. On day 5, you were challenged to ask and listen to God's wisdom in several areas of your life (p. 167). What answers did you receive? What did He say? How can we as a group help hold you accountable in these areas?

To close, call on girls to look back at page 167 where they asked for God's wisdom and direction in certain areas of their lives. Invite the girls to talk about a few of the areas in their lives where they think they most need God's wisdom and direction. As the girls identify common areas of concern, direct them to create groups based on those areas (friendship, future, relationships). Direct the girls to share prayer requests related to the area they chose, then close in prayer in those groups, praying by name for each person in the group.

❶ **If you want to get creative and like to cook, create a batch of fortune cookies** with Scripture references about wisdom included in each cookie. Deliver them to girls at home, through the mail, or bring them next week as a nice surprise.

❷ **Take note of girls who were struggling with major issues that need God's wisdom** (parent issues, boyfriend, and so forth). Take time to follow up with those girls (and possibly their parents) this week.

Faith Under Pressure: Constant

- Handheld mirrors for each girl
- Magazines
- Scissors
- Decoupage glue (like Mod-Podge® or a similar product, found at most craft stores)

WHAT TO DO:

This week, your group activity will take place at the end. To begin your time together, **explain that you all are going to dive into the debriefing questions right away.**

WHAT TO ASK:

Ask girls the following two questions, just as you have each week. As always, as girls answer the questions, take notes so that you can hold girls accountable for what God is doing in their lives:

1 **What was the most significant thing God said to you as you studied James this week?**

2 **What is God asking you to do as a result?**

WHAT TO DISCUSS:

Review the week by asking the following questions:

1. On Day 1 (p. 174), you evaluated your resources. What resources do you have that others could use (property, money, time, clothes, and so forth)? What steps are you taking to use the resources you have to help others?

2. What did you learn about the end result of self-indulgence during this week's study (p. 173-174)?

3. On Day 2, you learned about faithful followers of God. Who are some people you know personally who have persevered in the midst of trials or trouble? Tell their stories and explain why their perseverance encourages you.

4. Why is it important to remember God's character—who and what He is—in the middle of a time of suffering? Have you ever experienced the peace of trusting God and His character in the middle of a tough time? What did you learn?

5. On page 183, you graded yourself on your level of trustworthiness in the eyes of others. Which person did you think would have given you the highest grade? Lowest grade? Explain your answers.

6. On Day 4 (p. 186), you listed, described, or drew what you would say to an incoming class of students about how to have a thriving, active faith during their teen years. What were some of the things you said you would have pointed out? Why?

7. This week, you also learned about prayer. Did you learn anything new or surprising about prayer? How did this week's study change the way you pray?

8. How do you feel knowing that you help the weak and sick by praying for them?

9. What areas in your life are weak? Who can lift you up and encourage you? Why would you choose that person to encourage you?

10. On your last day of study this week, you talked about straying and wandering in your relationship with God (p. 191). What was it like to be in that place? What did you learn about yourself during that time? What did you learn about God? If you've experienced a time of wandering away from God, how does the way you felt during that time help you to understand and help those who might be straying from God now?

HOW TO END:

Explain that you'll end today's meeting by asking the girls to answer one question, but that their answers will come in the craft project. Distribute hand mirrors and craft supplies to each girl. **Explain that you'd like them to answer the following question by creating a collage on the back of the mirrors:** *Based on what you've discovered about James' life, writing, and ministry, what traits do you want others to see reflected in your life?*

Allow the girls sufficient time to work on their projects (they may complete them next week if necessary) and to share and explain what they've created.

To close the session, call the girls into a time of prayer, inviting each girl to voice a prayer for her own life based on her mirror project. If you'd like to create a prayer experience, direct the group to pray for each girl and the things of Christ she wants her life to reflect. Each girl should take a turn sitting in the center chair while the other girls place their hands on her and pray for her and her relationship with Christ.

WHAT TO DO AFTERWARD:

❶ **Next week's meeting will be different than the others and will require extra preparation.** Read ahead to begin gathering what you need.

❷ **Keep the decoupage supplies handy** in case girls need to complete their projects next week.

WEEK 8

☀ Faith Under Pressure: Thriving

WHAT TO BRING:

- Art supplies (glue, scissors, scrap paper, construction paper, markers, glitter, etc)
- Poster boards, cut in half (one half per girl)
- Snacks and drinks

WHAT TO DO:

This week's group time will be a little different. It will be a time for girls to reflect on and celebrate all that God did and continues to do in their lives as a result of studying the Book of James.

LIFEWAY GIRLS' CONFERENCE

Be challenged to change your world at our annual conference!

Teen girls and leaders will experience training and equipping, worship, breakouts, refreshment, and connection. We hope you will join us!

Want to know more?
lifeway.com/girls

LifeWay | Student

Before girls arrive, **set up the meeting space so that girls have a lot of room, but also have equal access to the art supplies,** which should be in a central location. If possible, you may want to bring in some extra card tables or other steady surfaces for more work space. Don't forget the drinks and snacks!

Explain to girls that they will be creating a poster to hang in their rooms as a reminder of how God worked in their lives over the last eight weeks. Stress that they can focus their poster on one truth or on several things God taught them, and their work can be as abstract or literal as they want. The point is simply that the girls have something tangible at the end of the session that they can see and be reminded of what God has taught them during this Bible study. This is an active way to remind girls to not just be hearers of the Word, but doers!

Allow the girls time to create their artwork, then **invite them to share their posters and the things God has done in their lives during this study.** You might also want to point out changes you see in girls' lives that they may not yet readily see. (You may want to look over the notes you've taken each week as the girls answered the two debriefing questions.)

HOW TO END:

When the girls' posters are complete, **direct each girl to sign the back of everyone else's poster.** Challenge the girls to write a short prayer on each poster that they sign.

To close, challenge each girl to voice a prayer to God. In that prayer, each should talk to God about the major theme(s) or truth(s) God revealed to her throughout the study. It can be a confession, praise, or a plea for help. After the girls have all prayed, pray for each one individually, asking God's blessing on the girls. Pray a unique blessing on each one according to her needs and life situation.

WHAT TO DO AFTERWARD:

1. **Get together with other leaders** (if necessary) to regroup and pray about the next steps for your small group.

2. **Continue to hold girls accountable to the life changes God is working in their lives.** This may involve coffee chats, Facebook updates, text messages, and so forth.

3. **Tell us about what God did in your group** through *James: Faith Under Pressure.* Email your comments to *mandy.crow@lifeway.com.* Also let us know how we can improve our resources to better meet your needs as a leader.